NONVIOLENT CRISIS INTERVENTION®

NONVIOLENT

CRISIS

INTERVENTION®

LEARNING TO DEFUSE
EXPLOSIVE BEHAVIOR

By
AlGene P. Caraulia
Linda K. Steiger

CPI Publishing
Brookfield, Wisconsin

ISBN 0-9651733-2-1

Printed in the United States of America

First Edition

DEDICATION

*This book is dedicated to the thousands
of Certified Instructors throughout the world
who teach Nonviolent Crisis Intervention.
Through their efforts the philosophy of care,
welfare, safety, and security
becomes reality.*

CONTENTS

NONVIOLENT CRISIS INTERVENTION®

INTRODUCTION

PEOPLE IN CRISIS. If you work in the field of human services —
as a teacher, a nurse, a social worker, a counselor, or any other
helping professional — you encounter them often. The angry
adolescent who strikes a teacher. The psychiatric patient who
engages in self-abuse. The agitated client who verbally abuses
staff members. The emotionally impaired child who constantly
hits and kicks. People in crisis.

Crises are narrow moments in time when a person is clearly
in need of supervision or protection. As staff members, we are
called upon to intervene with people in crisis in order to prevent
them from hurting themselves or others. A crisis requires our
immediate attention and response.

But how do we best respond to a person in crisis? Often, the
crisis situation is a chaotic one. Not only is a person in our charge
out of control, but staff members may lose control as well. Our
professional training often leaves us unprepared for dealing with
the person who has lost rational or physical control. We may

have learned theories about crisis behavior — but theories are of little use when we are attacked by someone we are supposed to be helping. For many of us, a crucial piece was left out of our education.

Nonviolent Crisis Intervention® — a training program developed by the Crisis Prevention Institute — provides the missing piece. It is a practical crisis management program that works. We know it works because the people who are using the program every day tell us so. Over the past fifteen years more than one million human service employees have been trained in *Nonviolent Crisis Intervention*. The program has been implemented in schools, residential facilities, hospitals, mental health settings, and correctional facilities. In all these environments — and others — *Nonviolent Crisis Intervention* has been successfully used to reduce the incidence of disruptive and assaultive behavior.

Why does *Nonviolent Crisis Intervention* work? It works for several reasons. It works because it takes the chaos of a crisis and organizes that chaos into recognizable stages. It works because it teaches staff the most effective way to respond at each of these crisis stages. And perhaps most important, it works because of the program's underlying philosophy: to provide for the care, welfare, safety, and security of everyone who is involved in a crisis situation. Care, welfare, safety, and security are not simply buzzwords that sound the right note in your policies and procedures. They are the basic underpinnings of this entire program. The primary goal of the verbal and the physical interventions taught in *Nonviolent Crisis Intervention* is safety: your safety, as well as the safety of those who are in your charge.

No book can substitute for an actual training program. The physical techniques taught in *Nonviolent Crisis Intervention* and discussed in Chapter Four are not shown in this book because they cannot be safely learned from drawings or photographs. You can, however, learn the basic principles of *Nonviolent Crisis Intervention* from this volume. You can improve your ability to recognize and prevent potential crises. You can sharpen your skills in defusing a crisis before violence occurs. You can feel more confident about keeping yourself and others safe when a person loses physical control.

In the Chinese language, the word "crisis" includes the character for the word "danger" plus the character for the word "opportunity." Without a doubt, crisis moments are times of danger. But they are also dynamic opportunities to facilitate growth and change in the people with whom you work. That, too, is an important part of *Nonviolent Crisis Intervention*.

We at the Crisis Prevention Institute hope you find this book a helpful and practical resource as you go about your important work — helping people.

CHAPTER ONE

CPI CRISIS DEVELOPMENT MODEL

FOR THE HUMAN SERVICE worker, the words "crisis" and "chaos" often seem synonymous. In a time of crisis, a person in your charge loses control. And in the chaotic moments that follow, it is not unusual for staff to lose some degree of control as well.

But a crisis is not really as unpredictable and disorganized as it seems on the surface, and staff response to a crisis does not have to be unpredictable or disorganized either.

When most of us think of a crisis, we probably think of the moment when a person releases a great deal of verbal or physical energy, such as yelling and swearing or hitting and kicking. But almost every crisis begins long before that moment.

The CPI Crisis Development Model is a way of understanding how a crisis situation evolves through a series of stages and how our response to each stage has an effect on the outcome.

This chapter provides you with a basic overview of the model.

Subsequent chapters are devoted to a more detailed look at each stage and show you how to apply the information to the students, patients, residents, or clients in your workplace.

The Anxiety Behavior Level

The first stage you observe when a person is becoming agitated is called Anxiety.

CPI CRISIS DEVELOPMENT MODEL

Crisis Development   **Staff Response**

1. Anxiety

Anxiety is a noticeable change or increase in a person's behavior. It is most observable through nonverbal communication. Let's take a common example: a person who is sitting in a waiting area in your facility. Whether it is a student waiting to see the principal, a client waiting to see a counselor, or a family member waiting for news from surgery, the act of waiting often produces anxiety.

By observing the behavior of the person who is waiting, we are able to see the anxiety. Some of the signs include:

- pacing • drumming the fingers
- fidgeting • wringing the hands
- rocking • playing with an object, like a paper clip or pen

All these are signs or indicators of anxiety: an increase in behavior which involves a nondirected or misdirected expenditure of energy. In other words, the person is accomplishing nothing through this behavior except burning up "nervous energy."

In some cases, a noticeable change in behavior means that a usually outgoing person becomes very quiet and withdrawn. This, too, can be a sign of anxiety, and one that is particularly easy to ignore. But ignoring anxiety is seldom a good strategy.

THE SUPPORTIVE RESPONSE

When a person is anxious, we, as staff, have our first and best opportunity to intervene and head off a potential crisis situation. The best response we can give to an anxious person is to be supportive.

CPI CRISIS DEVELOPMENT MODEL	
CRISIS DEVELOPMENT	**STAFF RESPONSE**
1. Anxiety	1. Supportive

A Supportive Response is one that acknowledges, and takes seriously, the concerns of the anxious person. A Supportive Response might be a word of reassurance, a smile, an offer to help, or simply a willingness to listen.

How we show support depends upon three things: (1) the type of support we are comfortable giving; (2) the type of support the other person responds to; and (3) the degree of rapport, if any, we share with that individual.

What is most important is that we demonstrate care and concern. It is easy to overlook the anxious person because she is not usually causing a disruption or overtly asking for our assistance. But when we do not pay attention to anxiety, we are missing an excellent opportunity to be proactive and prevent a potential crisis from developing further.

THE DEFENSIVE BEHAVIOR LEVEL

Although a high percentage of crisis situations can be defused at the Anxiety Level, some situations progress to the next Crisis Development Behavior Level.

This can happen for several reasons. Perhaps we failed to recognize the anxiety behavior; or we recognized it but believed we were too busy to intervene. Perhaps the person confronting us has already moved past the Anxiety Level, and we never had a chance for that early intervention. Or perhaps our Supportive Response was unsuccessful in calming the anxious person, and she escalated to the next behavior level: the Defensive Level.

CPI CRISIS DEVELOPMENT MODEL

Crisis Development	Staff Response
1. Anxiety	1. Supportive
2. Defensive	

At the Defensive Level, a person begins to lose rational control. She is not totally out of control, but she may be headed in that direction. Defensive behaviors include: questioning authority, noncompliance, yelling, name calling, and making threats.

Individuals at the Defensive Level are often so successful in pushing the buttons of staff members that staff also become defensive. When we become defensive ourselves, we allow the other person to control the interaction. This is a potentially dangerous situation.

Remember, this person is losing control and needs our assistance in regaining control. In fact, sometimes she is actively seeking such assistance. A defensive reaction on our part only feeds the other person's defensive behavior.

Similarly, the supportive approach recommended with an anxious person also may cause the defensive individual's behavior to escalate.

THE DIRECTIVE RESPONSE

The best way to provide assistance and help the individual regain control is to be directive.

CPI CRISIS DEVELOPMENT MODEL

CRISIS DEVELOPMENT	STAFF RESPONSE
1. Anxiety	1. Supportive
2. Defensive	2. Directive

Being directive means giving the person simple, clear instructions. What do we want the person to do? What do we want the person to stop doing? We need to give this information very clearly, remembering that the defensive individual is beginning to lose control and may not be processing information as well as he would under normal circumstances.

In addition to giving simple, clear instructions, the Directive Response to an individual may include setting limits. "Limit setting" is a term commonly used but often misunderstood. Setting a limit is not the same as issuing an ultimatum. "If you don't lower your voice, you will be confined to your room tonight" is an ultimatum, not a limit.

When you set a limit, you provide an individual with choices and consequences, and you do your best to help him make the positive choice. In the same situation, you might say, "If you lower your voice, you'll be able to participate in the recreation program this evening. If you don't lower your voice, you'll be confined to your room. So please keep it down; we've got a fun evening planned, and I'd really like you to be a part of it."

Effective limit setting emphasizes the positive choice, but ultimately it gives control to the defensive individual. The "how to" of effective limit setting is covered in Chapter Three.

THE ACTING-OUT PERSON

Despite our best efforts to intervene early and set effective limits, there are times when a person's behavior escalates beyond the Defensive Level. The Acting-Out Person Behavior Level occurs when a person totally loses control — rationally, emotionally, and physically. At this point, physical aggression usually occurs, and the person becomes a danger to self or to others.

CPI CRISIS DEVELOPMENT MODEL

CRISIS DEVELOPMENT	STAFF RESPONSE
1. Anxiety	1. Supportive
2. Defensive	2. Directive
3. Acting-Out Person	

It is most unlikely that the Acting-Out Person will respond to a supportive or directive staff attitude. In fact, this individual may not even hear the words spoken to her. Verbal intervention may no longer be an option.

NONVIOLENT PHYSICAL CRISIS INTERVENTION

At this point, it may be necessary to physically control the person's behavior until she is able to regain control. Nonviolent Physical Crisis Intervention is the recommended staff response.

CPI CRISIS DEVELOPMENT MODEL

CRISIS DEVELOPMENT	STAFF RESPONSE
1. Anxiety	1. Supportive
2. Defensive	2. Directive
3. Acting-Out Person	3. Nonviolent Physical Crisis Intervention

Nonviolent Physical Crisis Intervention consists of nonharmful restraint techniques to safely control an individual until she can regain control of her own behavior. It should be used only as a last resort.

Physical intervention, when it is used appropriately, can be as therapeutic as any other intervention tool. Initiating physical control for a person's own safety is another way of providing for the individual's care and welfare.

Tension Reduction

The fourth and final Crisis Development Level is Tension Reduction. It is a behavior level often overlooked in crisis development, but in many ways it is the most important.

During the development of a crisis, there is a tremendous build-up and expenditure of energy. This outburst of energy cannot last forever; eventually, every person will calm down. Tension Reduction occurs on both a physical and an emotional level as the individual begins to regain rational control.

CPI CRISIS DEVELOPMENT MODEL

Crisis Development	Staff Response
1. Anxiety	1. Supportive
2. Defensive	2. Directive
3. Acting-Out Person	3. Nonviolent Physical Crisis Intervention
4. Tension Reduction	

Losing control can be a frightening experience, and often the aftermath leaves people feeling embarrassed, scared, confused, or remorseful. On the other hand, it is also a time when people tend to be more open to the possibility of change. It can be a reachable, teachable moment.

THERAPEUTIC RAPPORT

Our response as staff members is crucial. When a person reaches the level of Tension Reduction, we have an opportunity to respond by re-establishing communication. This is called Therapeutic Rapport.

CPI CRISIS DEVELOPMENT MODEL

CRISIS DEVELOPMENT	STAFF RESPONSE
1. Anxiety	1. Supportive
2. Defensive	2. Directive
3. Acting-Out Person	3. Nonviolent Physical Crisis Intervention
4. Tension Reduction	4. Therapeutic Rapport

Therapeutic Rapport is a time for reviewing the crisis situation — why it happened, what led up to it, and, most important, how similar crises can be avoided in the future. This staff response, a part of our postvention, leads to an emphasis on prevention. We may not be able to eliminate all future crises, but we can look for ways to make them shorter, less intense, and less frequent.

INTEGRATED EXPERIENCE

The CPI Crisis Development Model is designed to help you, a human service professional, identify the behavior levels exhibited by the individuals in your charge and then respond appropriately. The goal is to avoid either overreacting or underreacting to the person's behavior.

Crisis development is an integrated experience because no one's behavior occurs in a vacuum. In other words, the behavior of the agitated, aggressive, or assaultive person affects us; and our behavior, in turn, affects the other person. We can influence the outcome of a potential crisis situation by the responses we choose.

For example, if we encounter a person at the Anxiety Level and we mirror his behavior with our own anxiety, we are likely to escalate the situation. The same holds true for defensive behavior. If a defensive individual becomes irrational and belligerent, and if we momentarily lose our professionalism and become defensive in return, we will probably be "adding fuel to the fire."

The objective is to offset or balance behavior. Anxious people need support, and defensive individuals require direction and limits. If a person totally loses control and acts out physically, she needs someone to physically maintain control to prevent her from harming herself or others. Finally, a person experiencing tension reduction needs therapeutic rapport.

SUMMARY

Crises don't just occur out of nowhere. Understanding the CPI Crisis Development Model can help you to recognize the early warning signs of a burgeoning crisis, to intervene without underreacting or overreacting, and to use the crisis as an opportunity for change and growth.

CHAPTER TWO

THE ANXIETY LEVEL: EARLY WARNING SIGNS

RECOGNIZING ANXIOUS BEHAVIOR early in the crisis development process and responding in a supportive manner is the best way to defuse a potentially explosive situation.

Most people would agree that early intervention, while the person is still rational, is more effective than intervening later, when the individual becomes irrational and possibly assaultive.

CPI CRISIS DEVELOPMENT MODEL

CRISIS DEVELOPMENT	STAFF RESPONSE
1. Anxiety	1. Supportive

Human service professionals often receive training in techniques designed to provide support to an anxious person. This formal training may include listening skills, interviewing methods, and counseling techniques. Each of these intervention strategies revolves around the exchange of words. Yet the skills which are often most effective in dealing with an anxious person involve a type of training that is frequently absent from the human service professional's repertoire: understanding and utilizing effective nonverbal communication.

THE ROLE OF NONVERBAL BEHAVIOR

Despite our highly developed language skills, as much as 80 percent of our communication is estimated to be nonverbal. In the context of intervening with a person experiencing anxiety, an acute awareness of nonverbal messages becomes essential.

PROXEMICS

Imagine being alone in an elevator. The doors of the elevator open and a person you've never met steps inside. Instead of retreating to the traditional "opposite corner," the stranger stands about a foot away from you. In addition, he doesn't cast his eyes up toward the numbers above the door, but pleasantly looks at you. This unusual behavior would be highly unsettling to most people. At a minimum, you would probably feel uncomfortable, and you might even be fearful that your safety may be threatened.

What is at work here is much more than simply rude or inappropriate social behavior. Few of us were taught by our parents to seek out the opposite corner of an elevator and stare at the numbers. In fact, we probably instinctively kept our distance in elevators before we had the language skills to comprehend a parental lesson in elevator etiquette.

When a person stands too close to us in an elevator, or when we approach too closely a person experiencing anxiety, a very powerful dynamic involving proxemics is triggered. Proxemics, or personal space as it is most commonly called, refers to the area around our bodies that we perceive as an extension of ourselves. Any encroachment on or invasion of that space tends to heighten anxiety. Generally, the distance we feel comfortable maintaining is two to three feet.

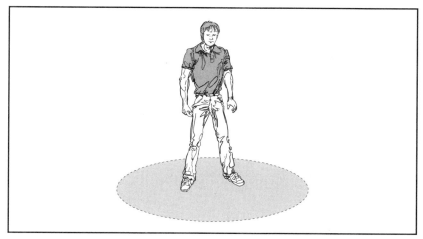

Fig. 1: Personal Space

This distance varies from person to person, as it does for the same person, depending on who is approaching and the context of the situation. For instance, if someone you knew and trusted approached you in a nonthreatening environment, your personal space would be much different than it would be if a stranger approached you on a city street late at night. We allow very few people to get much closer to us than two to three feet.

This dynamic becomes critical in a potential crisis situation. When approaching a person displaying anxiety behavior, keep in mind that he may not be as comfortable as you are with the situation. Pay close attention to the intensity of the anxiety behaviors. If the anxiety increases, you may need to back off a few steps. Maintaining a distance of two to three feet is a good rule of thumb; however, you should take your cues from the person you are approaching. Some people may need five to ten feet or more in order to feel comfortable in certain situations.

Being aware of an individual's need for personal space is one of the most critical keys to defusing a crisis, especially in the early stages of anxiety. Unfortunately, many crisis situations that could have been de-escalated are not, because of a staff member's invading a person's space. Often the staff member has good intentions. He may even want to give a supportive touch to the shoulder, thinking the anxious person needs a reassuring gesture. Such a gesture, however, not only might heighten anxiety, but also, in extreme cases, might be perceived as a threat and escalate the person to the point at which he becomes assaultive. Supportive touch can be an excellent therapeutic technique, but be sure you are taking your cues from the anxious person. Giving a person "space" can be just as therapeutic.

KINESICS

Narrowly defined, kinesics is the way we move and position our bodies. A broader application of the definition is more useful when intervening with a potentially disruptive individual. For our purpose, we will extend the definition of kinesics to mean our body language. The way we move and position our body in relation to another person has a direct impact on the message we deliver. Even subtle gestures add meaning to our words. For example, if we watch a scene on television with the sound turned down and see a scowling mother quickly approach her young child with her hands on her hips, we hardly need to turn up the volume to understand a good deal about her state of mind. We may not know the specifics, but we are relatively sure she is not about to lavish praise.

When we approach an anxious person, much of her anxiety is displayed by kinesic behavior. The very words we use to describe an anxious person reflect the fact that we are constantly reading body language. Phrases such as "uptight," "wound up," and "on edge" create visual images of people pacing, fidgeting, or wringing their hands. By "tuning in" to people's body language, we get some important cues about their levels of anxiety.

It is equally important when intervening in a crisis situation that we be aware of the message our body language is sending. Contrasting supportive words with negative body language can send a mixed message to the individual we are trying to calm. If, for example, a staff member approaches an anxious person head on, face to face, shoulder to shoulder, hands on hips while sighing and rolling her eyes, it will not make much difference what she says to the person. Her verbal message will be overridden by her inappropriate kinesic behavior.

We "read" people's bodies just as much as, if not more than, we listen to the words they speak. It is important to remember that a person in the early stages of crisis development may be even more acutely aware of our body language. If the intent is to present a supportive approach to the individual, we must be sure it is a consistent message, one that is supported by our nonverbal behavior as well as by our words.

THE CPI SUPPORTIVE STANCE

Since our nonverbal behavior plays such a major role in keeping anxiety to a minimum, we need to devise an approach that is nonthreatening or neutral in nature. The drawing on the next page demonstrates the CPI Supportive Stance.

For several reasons, this stance is recommended for approaching a person displaying anxiety behavior. First, by maintaining two to three feet of distance between yourself and the anxious person, you communicate a certain degree of respect by the fact

Fig. 2: CPI Supportive Stance

that you are honoring the individual's personal space. Remember, two to three feet is a guideline, not an absolute. You may not be able to get this close to some people. Take your cues from the person.

The second benefit of the CPI Supportive Stance is that by standing off to the side of the individual, you are presenting a nonthreatening, nonchallenging posture. When two people want to challenge each other, they generally "square off." This is true in almost all cases. It would be difficult to imagine an altercation in which this kinesic dynamic did not occur. It is highly unusual to see two people in a heated dispute in which one or both parties are maintaining a supportive stance.

Finally, this stance affords you much greater personal safety should the individual you are approaching become physically aggressive. The first safety factor built in to this stance is that you are providing a margin of at least one leg length of distance between you and the other individual. If the person tries to physically attack you, she must telegraph her assault by taking a step toward you. Also, by not squaring off with the individual, you are protecting the vulnerable areas of your body, such as your face, groin, knees, and shins.

Notice also in this stance that the hands of the staff member are in a neutral position and plainly in view. Keeping your hands in front of you puts them in a position to be used as shields, should the person strike out at you. Placing your hands behind your back is a good way to increase the other person's anxiety. Keep in mind that the person you are approaching may not be totally rational and could very well imagine you have something behind your back that could harm him.

The CPI Supportive Stance is the recommended posture for approaching a person who is displaying a significant amount of anxiety. It is also a sound way to position your body, regardless of where the individual is in the crisis development process. The fundamental dynamics that make it effective in defusing anxiety also apply to those individuals in the more volatile Defensive Level. And, as previously mentioned, you are physically safer in this position should the individual escalate to the level of physically acting out.

PARAVERBAL COMMUNICATION

A one-year-old child becomes frightened when he hears his parents quarreling. The same child gurgles with delight when a happy clown talks to him in a sing-song rhythmic manner on television. How can the child discriminate between the two situations before he develops the complex language skills to comprehend words? Part of the answer lies in the fact that the child is not reacting to words at all but is interpreting the communication on a much more primitive level. You could say the child is responding to the "flavor" of the interactions as opposed to the substance of the message. For instance, if you took the parents' quarrel and maintained the harsh, loud tones, but substituted kind words, odds are the child would still become frightened. Alternatively, if the happy clown smiles and merrily sings a tragic, heart-wrenching story, most likely you will find the child still chirping with delight.

Paraverbal communication is simply "how we say what we say." The manner in which we alter our tone, volume, and rate of speech affects the way our message is interpreted. The foregoing example illustrates the impact of paraverbal communication. Obviously, a one-year-old has limited verbal comprehension skills and, therefore, relies heavily on tone, volume, and rate of speech to gain context or meaning. The example points out, however, that we learn to interpret the subtleties of paraverbal communication long before we acquire complex language skills.

How does this dynamic apply to intervening with potentially disruptive and assaultive individuals? People in crisis situations, even in the early stages, begin to lose rationality. When this occurs, they respond to more basic levels of communication.

Recall for a moment a time when you became extremely upset. It is likely you will remember most vividly not the words that were exchanged, but the "flavor" of the exchange.

The tone, volume, and cadence of our speech provide a backdrop for our words. Take the simple phrase "calm down." By slightly altering the tone and volume of our voice we can substantially change our meaning. If we whine a little and stretch the phrase out until it has three or four syllables instead of only two, we can deliver a message that implies, "What are you so upset about? Your problems are trivial." Shorten our speech pattern and increase the volume, and we could give a totally different message that says, "I'm in charge, and I'm ordering you to calm down...or else!"

When intervening, be aware of the message your paraverbal communication sends. Coupled with nonverbal communication, paraverbals "package" your verbal intervention. Pay special attention to the tone of your voice. Although rate and volume are important, your tone tends to give your message a great deal of its meaning. If your intent is to provide support, make sure your tone is supportive. On the other hand, if you want to be directive, adjust your paraverbals accordingly. Try to keep your verbal, nonverbal, and paraverbal communication in sync with one another to avoid giving the person a mixed message.

SUMMARY

Anxiety is generally the first stage of crisis development. It is usually displayed by a noticeable increase or change in behavior. Often this behavior change is manifested by an increase in nonverbal behavior, such as pacing and finger-drumming. Recognizing anxiety and responding in a supportive manner are how most potential crisis situations are defused.

When you approach a person at any level of crisis development, it is suggested that the CPI Supportive Stance be used. This stance respects the person's personal space, avoids presenting a kinesic challenge to the individual, and provides a margin of personal safety for you should the individual physically act out.

Try to be acutely aware of your paraverbal communication. Your voice, including its tone, volume, and rate of speech, significantly affects the meaning behind your words. Your verbal, nonverbal, and paraverbal communication should be consistent with the message you want to deliver.

CHAPTER THREE

THE DEFENSIVE LEVEL: HOSTILITY AND NONCOMPLIANCE

IF ALL CRISIS SITUATIONS could be defused at the Anxiety Level, there would be very little need for this book. Life would be much simpler if we had to worry only about the most effective ways to be supportive. Some crisis situations, however, escalate past the Anxiety Level into the more volatile Defensive Level. When individuals become defensive, they lose rationality and often become difficult to handle.

Many people find it extremely challenging to manage defensive behavior. A person in the Defensive Level begins to lose control. Often this loss of control is accompanied by belligerence, hostility, and noncompliance. The person who was nervous and edgy during the Anxiety Level now becomes extremely volatile and is not so easily approached. Often, the defensive person will challenge you or your authority.

Typically, this behavior is characterized by verbal outbursts. In some cases, however, the person may become passively noncompliant and refuse to accommodate even the simplest request.

Supportive responses that work well with people who are anxious lose much of their effectiveness with the defensive person. This can lead to frustration on the part of staff.

A directive approach, which provides structure and choices, is generally much more effective with a person in the Defensive Level.

CPI CRISIS DEVELOPMENT MODEL

CRISIS DEVELOPMENT	STAFF RESPONSE
1. Anxiety	1. Supportive
2. Defensive	2. Directive

With a directive approach, unlike the supportive approach, you set limits for the individual and clearly establish consequences for the defensive behavior.

THE CPI VERBAL ESCALATION CONTINUUM

Defensive behavior seems chaotic and unpredictable, often with no apparent pattern. However, there are certain behaviors commonly observed when individuals become defensive.

The CPI Verbal Escalation Continuum is designed to identify the behaviors most often seen with a person who is in the Defensive Level. The model allows you to break down the seemingly unlimited number of behaviors into five distinct and identifiable categories. The intent is not to oversimplify behavior; instead, the model allows us to develop a manageable number of strategies.

Granted, not all defensive behaviors fall neatly into one of five categories. You will find, however, that the model provides an excellent framework for responding to most defensive behaviors.

QUESTIONING

Generally, questioning is one of the first behaviors you see in a person who is escalating in the Defensive Level.

THE VERBAL ESCALATION CONTINUUM

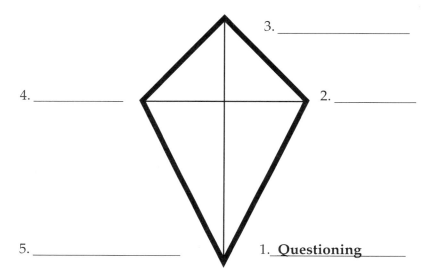

3. _____

4. _____

2. _____

5. _____

1. **Questioning** _____

Questioning can take one of two forms. The first is information-seeking in nature. These are productive questions and usually are asked to clarify information. For example, if you direct a person to leave an unauthorized area, he may ask you why he cannot continue to stay in the area. Do not assume a person understands why your directive is being issued. When a question appears to be informational, give the person the benefit of the doubt and answer the question. He may not know why he has to leave an area, take medication, or lower his voice. In many cases, explanation and clarification are all that is necessary. Once the person receives more information, he will comply with your directive.

The second type of questioning, however, is not so straight-forward. At times people question your directive in order to challenge you. Such questions may be disguised as information seeking, but they actually have little to do with gaining information. For example, if you ask an individual to lower her voice, a typical challenge question might be, "What gives you the right to tell me what to do?"

This type of question does not seek information. Instead, it attempts to challenge you and your authority. By trying to answer a challenge question as you would answer an information-seeking question, you may end up defending yourself and, as a result, losing credibility.

Another common pitfall in trying to answer challenge questions as if they were information-seeking is that your interaction strays from the original directive.

Consider the following dialogue:

Staff:	It's time to leave the day room and head to the recreation area.
Defensive Person:	It's only two o'clock. I thought I didn't have to go until three.
Staff:	No. Rec hour begins at two.
Defensive Person:	You've only worked here three months. You don't even know the rules. Who told you the rules here?
Staff:	I was trained by Mr. Peters.

Defensive Person:	Oh, Peters. He doesn't know anything. How come he trained you? Doesn't Johnson do orientation?
Staff:	Well, yes, he usually does.
Defensive Person:	Everything's always so damn screwed up around here. If you guys would just have some consistency, things might work.

This verbal exchange is an exaggerated example of how challenge questions can divert an issue away from the original directive. The best response to a challenge question is to refocus the attention back to the issue at hand — in this case, the individual moving to the recreation area. The more focus you can maintain on the specific directive, the better chance you have of gaining compliance.

Staff:	It's time to leave the day room and head to the recreation area.
Defensive Person:	It's only two o'clock. I thought I didn't have to go until three.
Staff:	No. Rec hour begins at two.
Defensive Person:	You've only worked here three months. You don't even know the rules. Who told you the rules here?
Staff:	Rec hour begins at two. It's time to leave.
Defensive Person:	(pause) Okay.

REFUSAL

The next stage commonly observed in a person who is verbally escalating is refusal.

THE VERBAL ESCALATION CONTINUUM

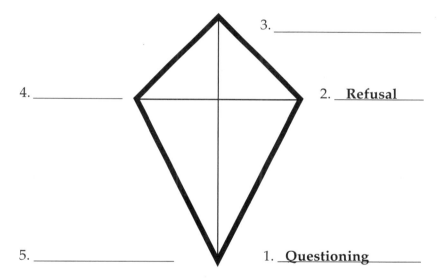

3. _____

4. _____

2. **Refusal**

5. _____

1. **Questioning**

The refusal stage of the continuum is characterized by outright noncompliance. The individual with whom you are being directive simply refuses to do what you ask her to do.

It is easy to become frustrated at this point. In some cases, you may feel that if you cannot convince the person to comply, you have failed in your intervention. The reality is that you cannot make anyone do anything she has made up her mind not to do. Refusal is often the point at which the classic power struggle develops. Unfortunately, this is a "no win" situation.

The appropriate response to refusal is to set limits with the individual. Setting limits involves clearly pointing out to the person that she has choices to make. Also clearly point out that those choices have consequences. You must let the individual know that the choices are hers to make, not yours. The basic keys to setting limits are to be sure your limits are clear, simple, reasonable, and enforceable. Limit setting is further addressed later in this chapter.

RELEASE

The third stage of the continuum is verbal release.

THE VERBAL ESCALATION CONTINUUM

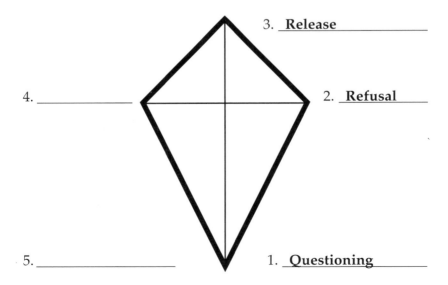

3. **Release**

4. _____

2. **Refusal**

5. _____

1. **Questioning**

Release is simply an outpouring of verbal energy. At this point, the individual might be screaming at the top of his lungs. During verbal release you may hear profanity, insults, and verbal irrationality.

During the release stage, keep in mind that if you respond verbally, the individual probably will not hear your words. At best, he will only partially process your verbal intervention. Unfortunately, this can cause a staff member to raise the volume of his voice to match the volume of the defensive person. This accomplishes little other than escalating the situation.

A person who is verbally releasing does not have an infinite amount of energy to expend. Sooner or later he will "run out of steam" and experience an energy lull. If possible, allow the person to expend and vent some energy. Since he will not hear most of what you are saying during the peak of energy output, you have few alternatives.

As the energy drops in intensity, attempt to restate your directive. Obviously, you cannot allow a person to go on indefinitely screaming at an ear-splitting decibel level. You will find, however, that most people will not be able to keep up a maximum energy output for very long. Most individuals will ultimately calm down, giving you an opportunity to interact with them on a more rational level.

INTIMIDATION

Intimidation is the next stage on the continuum.

THE VERBAL ESCALATION CONTINUUM

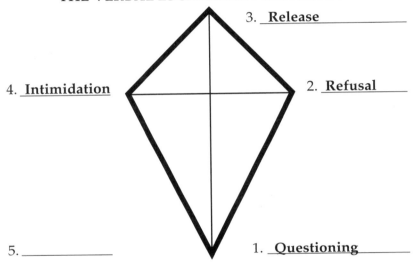

3. **Release**

2. **Refusal**

4. **Intimidation**

5. _____

1. **Questioning**

Intimidation is the point at which an individual threatens you in some manner. This could be in the form of a verbal or a nonverbal threat to your safety. Although many threats are not acted upon, you should take the threat seriously. Treat the threat as if it could be carried out.

Assess the nature of the threat. If it is not a threat to your personal safety, you may choose to continue your intervention and inform the individual of the consequences should she carry out the threat. For example, a person may threaten to tell your supervisor you are treating her unfairly. This obviously is not a threat to your personal safety and would be treated differently than a threat to your life.

If you are alone and feel the threat is of potential danger to your personal safety, you are wise to consider removing yourself from the situation. In these instances it is best to call in some assistance to handle the situation. How to quickly summon a team of two or more staff is discussed in a later chapter.

TENSION REDUCTION

Many verbally escalating situations conclude with Tension Reduction.

THE VERBAL ESCALATION CONTINUUM

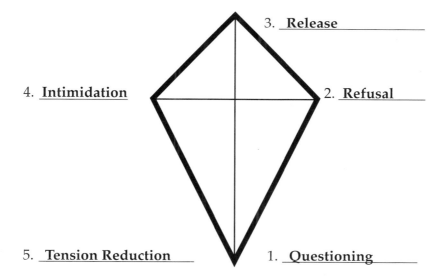

3. **Release**

4. **Intimidation**

2. **Refusal**

5. **Tension Reduction**

1. **Questioning**

Tension Reduction is the point at which the individual begins to regain rationality. As pointed out in Chapter One, the reduction in tension is both physical and emotional. This level is often characterized by embarrassment and remorse. Tension reduction provides an excellent opportunity for communication to occur.

Once the individual has regained rationality, it becomes much easier to talk with the person and, hopefully, effect some positive resolution to the incident. Communication with a person in the Tension Reduction stage is called Therapeutic Rapport, and that is the focus of Chapter Five.

The Verbal Escalation Continuum is a working model of the behaviors you will frequently observe in a defensive person. Although the stages are numbered from one to five, the model does not mean that a person will progress in sequence from one to another. Human behavior is not so predictable. A person may begin with questioning, proceed directly to the release stage, go back to refusal, and return again to questioning.

The value of the model does not lie in its ability to predict behavior in a sequential pattern. Instead, it provides a framework for you to design specific intervention strategies, depending on where the person is in the verbal escalation process. These responses are designed to maximize the chances of effecting Tension Reduction at any of the stages on the continuum.

SETTING LIMITS

Several times in this chapter we use the term "setting limits." Limit setting is the fundamental cornerstone of maintaining a directive approach. Stated simply, limit setting is the process by which you inform an individual of the choices he has regarding compliance with a directive you have issued. The second step of the process involves informing the individual of the consequences that will occur depending upon his choice.

THE KEYS TO SETTING LIMITS

Setting limits is probably one of the single most difficult tasks in a human service professional's daily responsibilities. Whether you are a teacher, a nurse, a child care worker, a counselor, a supervisor, or a parent, setting limits can be tough. Certain individuals seem to carry an aura of confidence and have very little problem being directive, but many of us struggle.

Not everyone can master the art of setting limits. Most people, however, can improve their limit-setting abilities through on-the-job experience. The individuals who are highly effective in limit setting have unique styles of managing behavior; however, they use certain underlying principles when setting limits.

Set limits that are clear. If you are not specific when you establish a limit, you have less chance of the individual complying. For example, suppose a person is using vulgar language and you need to inform her that the language is inappropriate.

You have a much greater chance of gaining compliance if you are specific in your directive. Avoid using general phrases such as "your behavior is inappropriate." Which behavior is inappropriate? Don't assume the person knows; be specific. Say: "Your language is offensive and violates the rules of this facility."

Set limits that are simple. Complex limits do not work very well. Keep in mind that the individual with whom you are working may not be rational. Giving a person four or five different choices when he is in a crisis may only confuse and escalate the situation. Generally, the simpler the limit, the more effective.

Set limits that are reasonable. Setting a limit that is unreasonable or unenforceable is a sure way to escalate a situation. Most people in your care know what you can and cannot do. If, for example, you impose stricter limits than your facility or organization allows, the individual may challenge you on the basis of your not being able to enforce the consequences. Reasonable limits go hand in hand with reasonable policies and procedures. Be sure the limits you impose are parallel to your organization's policies.

Set limits you will enforce. Before setting any limit, take a moment to ask yourself: Will I be prepared to enforce the consequences of this limit? It is human nature to test limits. You must be prepared to enforce the consequences, or your limit is meaningless. The individuals who are most effective in setting limits are those who follow through with consequences.

A FIVE-STEP APPROACH TO SETTING LIMITS

Setting limits with a noncompliant individual is anything but a science. There are many variables to take into account, including the type of person who is being noncompliant, the specific behavior for which you are setting limits, your skills and ability in enforcing consequences, and the context of the situation. Although each situation is different, several steps should be followed in virtually every situation requiring limit setting. The following five steps can be used as guidelines to follow.

1. Explain exactly which behavior is inappropriate. Be specific. Don't assume the individual knows which behavior is inappropriate. If, for example, a person is playing his radio too loudly, try to avoid generalizing, as in, "It's too noisy in here." Instead, focus on precisely what you want the person to do. In this example, a response such as, "Your radio is too loud. Can you please turn the volume down?" is much more direct. The more specific you can be, the less chance there is of misinterpretation.

2. Explain why the behavior is inappropriate. Do not assume that the individual knows why the behavior you are limiting is inappropriate. In the radio example, this may mean informing the individual that the loud music is disturbing others in the area. Most rules have some rationale behind them. Often those asked to abide by rules are not aware of why a rule is in place.

3. Give reasonable choices and consequences. Let the individual know he has choices. Try to emphasize the positive choice so it does not sound like an ultimatum. Using the radio example, you might want to let the person know that if he turns the radio down he can continue to play it. Try to emphasize the fact that the choices and their consequences are the individual's responsibility. People like to have options. Make sure the individual fully understands that he can determine the outcome of the situation.

4. Allow time to choose. Keep in mind that a verbally escalating person is probably somewhat irrational. The person may need a little time to sort out the choices and make a decision. Allow a reasonable amount of time for the person to make that decision. By allowing the person a little time, you are reinforcing the fact that it is his choice, not an ultimatum you are imposing.

5. Enforce consequences. None of your limits will be effective unless you are prepared to enforce your consequences. Often, the individual will be waiting to see if you are going to follow through.

This five-step process is the underlying formula used by most individuals who are consistently effective in setting limits. The goal of this approach is to structure limits so they can be given as choices, not mandated as ultimatums.

EMPATHIC LISTENING

At least fifty percent of our task when verbally intervening is listening. Unfortunately, we often pay more attention to what we are going to say than to actively listening to what the other person is saying. In many cases our minds drift and lose focus. We become distracted by external stimuli. In other cases our inward thought process interferes with our efforts to listen empathically. Often we are simply too preoccupied, preparing our response to what the other person is saying.

To verbally defuse a person's hostility we have to first and foremost listen with empathy. We have to try to understand what the other person is saying and how she is feeling about what she says. Good listeners have a profound calming effect on people. This is true regardless of whether the person is a trained psychoanalyst or a bartender.

Empathic listening is an active process requiring intense concentration and effort. Hearing is different from listening. When we hear someone say something, a series of sound waves strikes our eardrums causing nerves to send electrochemical impulses to our brain. When we listen, on the other hand, we involve a multitude of additional steps to process the information we receive. For example, if we listen empathically, we probably are doing as much listening with our eyes as we are with our ears. In order to empathize with what another person is feeling, we must listen to the "holistic expression" of their message, not merely their words. Empathic listening involves listening, as much as possible, from the other person's point of view.

THE FIVE KEYS TO EMPATHIC LISTENING

1. Avoid being judgmental. To listen with empathy, you must listen, not advise. This is not the time to give advice, offer counsel, determine who is right or wrong, or determine how serious the issue is. Empathy and criticism are opposite extremes. Empathy attempts to unconditionally understand another's point of view. Criticism, on the other hand, evaluates the validity of another's point of view. If it is your responsibility to make a judgment, bite your tongue and withhold both judgment and consequences for behavior until a more opportune moment to render a decision presents itself. Remember, you want to defuse a potentially hostile person. Trying to understand how he feels is a wiser prescriptive approach at this time than passing judgment.

2. Give your undivided attention. Most people, even young children, can tell when we are not paying attention to them. Focusing intently on what is being said not only allows you a better opportunity to feel what is being said, but also has a calming effect on the person with whom you are intervening. The quickest method known to enrage another person is to ignore him. Listening empathically takes intense concentration and is ineffective if the person listening is distracted by internal or external interference.

3. Focus on feelings. When listening empathically, listen for meaning. This requires paying close attention to feelings as well as facts. Try to listen for subtle underlying messages. Often, they are disguised by surface issues. Listen for underlying unmet needs. The underlying messages are often conveyed through nonverbal and paraverbal signals. Try to listen to the tone of voice, which is often a much clearer indicator of affect than words are.

4. Use silence. Silence is probably the most valuable technique used in empathic listening. Unfortunately, we are socialized to approach conversations as if they were tennis matches. When someone speaks to me, it is expected that I will respond immediately after he has spoken. This "volleying" effect may be suitable for everyday conversations when both people are rational. However, in situations involving a person who is escalating in a crisis, verbally responding to every statement can be a mistake. Silence, on the other hand, can be used to allow the person time to vent emotions, clarify meaning, and regain rationality.

5. Use restatement. Restatement, or "reflective questioning," is an extremely valuable way to assist the person and you in understanding the real meaning behind the words he is using. Often, during a crisis, an individual emotes feelings in the form of statements, not even realizing what is being said. Restating his phrases can help the individual clarify and organize his thoughts. In addition, restatement assists you in verifying that you have not misunderstood what the individual is really saying.

The following example illustrates how restatement can be valuable in clarifying meaning for both parties:

Person Escalating: I can't stand this place. No one gives me any respect around here!

Staff: So you don't feel you're treated fairly?

Person Escalating: That's what I said, didn't I?

Staff: (silence)

Person Escalating: No one tells me anything in this damn place.

Staff: Is there some information you feel you're not getting?

Person Escalating: Well, yeah!

Staff: (silence)

Person Escalating: It's just...uh....Why did they change the day room hours? Always messing with changes (pause). How's my dad gonna visit me now? He can't get over here during these new hours.

This is a simple yet common example of effective use of restatement and silence to listen empathically to the individual. The initial statement of "no respect" ended up as only a surface statement. Through the use of restatement and silence, the staff member discovered that the real issue was the individual's fear that his father would not be able to visit him.

SUMMARY

The second level in the CPI Crisis Development Behavior Level Model is the Defensive Level, characterized by the beginning stages of loss of rationality. Defensive individuals often become belligerent and hostile, and challenge you and your authority. A directive approach is the most effective staff response at this level and involves setting clear, reasonable, and enforceable limits.

The five keys to setting limits are:

1. Explain exactly which behavior is inappropriate.
2. Explain why the behavior is inappropriate.
3. Give the individual clear choices.
4. Allow time.
5. Enforce consequences.

One of the important elements critical to successful verbal intervention is empathic listening. Listening with empathy is an active process and involves avoiding being judgmental, giving undivided attention, focusing on feelings as well as facts, and using silence and restatement.

CHAPTER FOUR

THE ACTING-OUT PERSON: WHEN HOSTILITY TURNS TO VIOLENCE

THUS FAR WE HAVE EXAMINED the Crisis Development Behavior Levels through the Anxiety and Defensive Levels. In both of these stages, the person escalating still maintains a certain degree of control over his behavior.

Although an individual in the Defensive Level may be extremely irrational, he still maintains enough rationality to avoid physically acting out his verbal aggression.

CPI CRISIS DEVELOPMENT MODEL

CRISIS DEVELOPMENT	STAFF RESPONSE
1. Anxiety	1. Supportive
2. Defensive	2. Directive

In some cases, however, the energy build-up becomes so intense that a person does lose control and become physically aggressive. This is the point at which verbal defensiveness explodes into physical hostility, and the individual attempts to physically assault others or possibly harm himself. Supportive and directive verbal intervention is no longer adequate to calm down the situation, and other measures have to be taken before verbal intervention can resume its effectiveness.

NONVIOLENT PHYSICAL CRISIS INTERVENTION

When a person totally loses control and physically acts out, have we failed in our efforts to defuse the crisis? Some would say "yes," pointing to the fact that therapeutic verbal defusing efforts have failed. They say that when a person gets to the point at which he is physically out of control, he should be restrained, medicated, and secluded until he is calmed down. Only then can the therapeutic process be resumed.

There are two flaws in this thinking. First, to assume that you have failed if a person escalates to the point of physical aggression is a fallacy. Though most situations can be defused prior to that point, some individuals will escalate regardless of your intervention strategies.

Second, if a person acts out physically, to assume that you have failed in the therapeutic process **excludes physical acting out as a part of the crisis process**. Flailing, punching, kicking, and choking are the epitome of a crisis. Why should the therapeutic process be abandoned at the apex of crisis development?

Nonviolent Physical Crisis Intervention is a continuation of the therapeutic process that may have begun as early as the Anxiety Level. Physically taking control of another person's body and keeping her safe while not hurting her is possibly the most therapeutic act one can imagine.

CPI CRISIS DEVELOPMENT MODEL

CRISIS DEVELOPMENT	STAFF RESPONSE
1. Anxiety	1. Supportive
2. Defensive	2. Directive
3. Acting-Out Person	3. Nonviolent Physical Crisis Intervention

WHEN SHOULD NONVIOLENT PHYSICAL CRISIS INTERVENTION BE USED?

Often, staff members who encounter physical acting-out behavior ask the question, "When should physical restraint be used?" In some cases, the question they really want answered is, "When shouldn't we use physical restraint?" Due to the litigious nature of our society, liability is always a major concern when the issue of physical restraint is addressed.

Asking a question such as "When should we restrain a person?" is like asking "Should I brake or accelerate when approaching a traffic light that turns yellow?" Ask ten people and you will get ten different answers. The question is not a black and white issue; it involves many variables, including the training and skill of the individuals involved, the specific situation, and a great deal of professional judgment.

As a general policy guideline, the following serves well:

> *Nonviolent Physical Crisis Intervention should be used only as a last resort, after all other verbal intervention efforts have been exhausted, and only when the individual presents a danger to himself or others.*

This definition provides structure and guidelines for staff, as well as sufficient flexibility for professional judgment to be applied to each situation.

THE DANGERS OF A HANDS-OFF POLICY

Physically restraining a person is dangerous. It can lead to serious injury and, in extreme cases, death. It is no wonder that administrators are hesitant to train staff in how to physically restrain another person.

This fear of injury, death, and subsequent litigation leads some administrations to adopt a "hands-off" policy. Such a policy usually means that if a person should become physically assaultive, the staff are to remove themselves from the immediate situation and call for assistance, such as law enforcement.

This policy sounds reasonable. In many cases removing yourself from a situation is the best alternative for everyone involved. Law enforcement officers have more training to handle violent situations, they usually respond in teams, and they carry weapons, if necessary.

However, there are some dangers inherent in a hands-off policy. To start with, a hands-off policy implies conditional care during a crisis. It says to staff and potentially acting-out persons, "We will intervene in your crisis to ensure your care up to a point. If you move past that point and your behavior becomes too disordered, we will no longer provide for your care, welfare, safety, and security." Although this may be the best course of action when a person enters the front doors of a school threatening to use a shotgun, it is not the most appropriate policy in other situations, such as when two adolescents are fighting.

The problem arises when the policy is absolute. Facilities that adopt an absolute hands-off policy are telling staff it is policy to walk away from many situations. This presents an ethical concern as to where a professional's obligations start and end, as well as a legal concern involving potential negligence. The more practical problem with a hands-off policy is that it does not address situations in which an acting-out person assaults a staff member. Hands-off policies usually result in staff that are not properly trained in the safe management of assaultive behavior. Without training, what should a staff member do if assaulted?

Some facilities are hesitant to put staff through such training because of the concern that the physical techniques will be misused. This is dangerous logic.

If people are not trained, they usually have very little confidence. Lack of confidence can lead to fear. If staff are fearful of being physically assaulted, that can lead to overreaction. Without training, a normal human reaction if you are assaulted is to defend yourself. Self-defense usually equates to doing whatever is necessary to avoid being injured, and this often results in harm to the other party, as well as to yourself.

An absolute hands-off policy can lead to injury and litigation. It is analogous to not teaching a person how to use a fire hose lest she flood the building while putting out a fire. On the other hand, a modified hands-off policy, tempered by staff training and good contingency planning, can be quite effective.

The Appropriate Use of Nonviolent Physical Intervention

Physical intervention should be implemented to achieve only one goal: keeping the acting-out person and others in the area, including yourself, safe. It must be stressed when training staff that physical intervention has a singular purpose — to temporarily take control of another person until she can regain control of her own behavior. This may take five seconds, a minute, or ten minutes, depending on the length of time the individual is out of control.

Physical restraint should never be used as a punitive measure. In addition to the legal and ethical problems, punishing a person by restraining her does not curb future acting-out behavior.

Take, for example, techniques that are pain inflicting. There are a whole series of techniques borrowed from the martial arts that inflict pain without causing injury. The practical dilemma of using a pain-inflicting technique is that it actually promotes more acting-out behavior in the future.

When a person loses control and physically acts out, he often does not remember what happened during the loss of control. Often he regains his memory in the middle of a restraining procedure. If a person does not remember going out of control, and the first sensation he has when he regains control is pain, he will likely feel as if the staff has taken advantage of him. It is important to remember that when a person physically loses control, he is in a very emotionally vulnerable state. If you take care of his physical well-being during this vulnerable time, you will have a much greater chance of developing rapport once he has calmed down. If pain is inflicted, on the other hand, he will most likely view you as an adversary, at best, and as a target for future aggression in a worst-case scenario.

Physical restraint used as punishment or administered in a painful manner may temporarily put a stop to physical acting-out behavior. It will be extremely difficult, however, to establish any postvention therapeutic rapport with the individual because the therapeutic process was abandoned in the middle of the crisis at the time the individual was most vulnerable.

WHEN SHOULD NONVIOLENT PHYSICAL CRISIS INTERVENTION END?

How long should you physically restrain a person? How do you know when it is safe to stop? Your physical restraint should last only as long as the physical acting-out behavior itself. There are no guidelines or averages to follow. Most people who physically act out do so for a brief period of time. The more securely they are restrained, the more likely they are to calm down quickly.

Generally, a person will struggle and rest, struggle and rest, with the intensity of her struggling diminishing as time goes on.

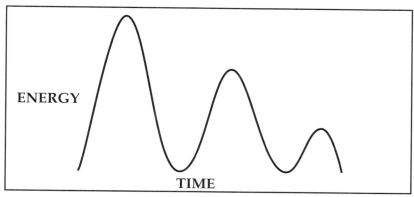

Fig. 3: Energy Expenditure

It is important to continue your verbal intervention efforts throughout the restraining process. Because you cannot be sure when the individual will regain her rationality, you should continually attempt to re-establish communication by talking with the person while restraining her. Reassure the individual. Let her know she is all right and that you are not going to hurt her. Keep in mind that the person you are restraining may not remember what has happened just prior to being restrained and is probably very frightened.

When the individual's energy level begins to subside, you begin to feel an actual reduction of tension in the person's body. The struggling becomes less intense, and you feel the muscles begin to relax. Keep talking to the person. As the energy subsides, you will notice an emotional tension reduction paralleling the physical tension reduction. Rage and cursing may transform into statements of remorse accompanied by sobbing.

Have the individual take some deep breaths. This serves two functions. First, breathing facilitates the process of calming down. Also, by directing the individual to take deep breaths, you are testing her rationality. If she complies, she has probably regained much of her rational thought process. Tell the individual exactly what is going to happen now. Remember that she is frightened. If you are going to release your restraint, negotiate an agreement that this will be done only if she remains calm. If you are going to walk with her to another area to talk, let her know where you are going and what you intend to do when you get there.

Be prepared for another physical outburst. Often when a restraint technique is released, the individual begins to physically act out again. If this happens, resume the restraint and repeat the negotiating process once the individual again appears calm.

SUMMARY

Nonviolent Physical Crisis Intervention involves safe restraint and is the appropriate response to an individual who is physically acting out. It is part of the therapeutic process and is used only as a last resort when the physically acting-out individual presents a danger to himself or others. Physical intervention is used only long enough for the individual to regain control of his behavior — never as a punitive measure. As control is regained, the individual moves to the final Crisis Development Behavior Level: Tension Reduction.

CHAPTER FIVE

TENSION REDUCTION:
AFTER THE CRISIS

DURING THE DEVELOPMENT OF A CRISIS, a tremendous amount of energy is built up and then expended by the Acting-Out Person. This high level of energy output cannot be sustained indefinitely; eventually, the person's energy dissipates, and the individual begins to calm down. This final behavior level in crisis development is referred to as Tension Reduction.

CPI CRISIS DEVELOPMENT MODEL

CRISIS DEVELOPMENT	STAFF RESPONSE
1. Anxiety	1. Supportive
2. Defensive	2. Directive
3. Acting-Out Person	3. Nonviolent Physical Crisis Intervention
4. Tension Reduction	

The response to a person experiencing Tension Reduction is part of a process called postvention. Postvention refers to staff actions during the aftermath of a crisis. One important part of postvention is re-establishing communication with the person who has acted out.

This means of re-establishing communication is called Therapeutic Rapport.

CPI CRISIS DEVELOPMENT MODEL

CRISIS DEVELOPMENT	STAFF RESPONSE
1. Anxiety	1. Supportive
2. Defensive	2. Directive
3. Acting-Out Person	3. Nonviolent Physical Crisis Intervention
4. Tension Reduction	4. Therapeutic Rapport

It takes place at a time when staff have a notable opportunity to intervene in a way that may prevent the next crisis — or at least reduce the frequency, duration, or intensity of subsequent crises. This is the final step in providing an individual with care, welfare, safety, and security.

A second part of postvention involves the Tension Reduction that is experienced by staff members — who have also expended a great deal of energy during the crisis! Crisis response team members will benefit from an opportunity to communicate with one another through a staff debriefing. Debriefing allows team members to discuss both the facts and their feelings surrounding the crisis incident.

THE CPI COPING MODEL

The CPI COPING Model is a tool to assist in the postvention process. The word COPING is a reminder that people often end up in crisis situations because they lack the necessary skills to cope with their feelings of anger, frustration, or fear in healthier ways. The word COPING also reminds us, as staff members, that we are focusing on ways to increase our ability to cope with crisis situations in a safe, therapeutic manner.

In addition, each letter of the word COPING stands for another word that describes a method for establishing Therapeutic Rapport, as well as for conducting a staff debriefing. The model looks like this:

CONTROL

ORIENT

PATTERNS

INVESTIGATE

NEGOTIATE

GIVE

First, let's apply the CPI COPING Model to postvention with the acting-out individual.

ESTABLISHING THERAPEUTIC RAPPORT

The interval of time after a crisis is often a period of vulnerability for the person who acted out. The individual is usually emotionally and physically drained. Feelings of remorse, fear, or shame may be expressed. The person is likely to be open to change at this time more so than at any other time.

It is important to remember, however, that our ability to capitalize on this opportunity to promote growth and change depends, in part, on how we handled our interactions with the person before and during the crisis. If, for instance, we became verbally abusive to the person or used a physical restraint when it was not warranted, it will be far more difficult to establish a therapeutic relationship with that person after the crisis.

The process of establishing Therapeutic Rapport is usually best accomplished by a staff person who was directly involved in the crisis incident. This person does not need to be a highly trained mental health professional. The postvention process takes place during a brief window of time after the crisis occurs. It is not a substitute for therapy or counseling; in fact, referral to such resources may be one of the outcomes of the process.

Here are the steps in establishing Therapeutic Rapport.

CONTROL

During a crisis, control is lost by the person who acted out, and sometimes by staff members, as well. Even in the case of an individual who has become defensive, but not physically violent, some rational control is lost. Before a crisis can be discussed, everyone needs to be back in control.

Staff members can determine if an individual has, in fact, regained control by assessing several nonverbal and verbal indicators of her status. Have her breathing and coloring returned to normal? Does she appear more relaxed? Is she able to communicate rationally? Does she respond appropriately to your words? Is she willing to comply with simple requests, such as "take a few deep breaths" or "sit down and rest a few minutes"?

Don't forget that you need to be back in control, too. If you are feeling angry with the individual, embarrassed by how you responded to the situation, or frightened that the person may re-escalate at any moment, you may not yet be ready to discuss the incident with the individual. Give yourself some time to calm down, as well.

There is no specific time period for achieving control. It depends on the people involved and on the seriousness of the incident which occurred. The time frame could be a few minutes, a few hours — or even the next day.

ORIENT

At this stage, after determining that everyone is back in emotional and physical control, determine — with the acting-out individual — just what happened. Orient yourself to the facts.

Let the person who acted out tell her side of the story first. Listen without question or comment, but with attentive body language. Model good listening behavior. After you have heard her entire story, ask clarifying questions, but try to remain nonjudgmental. If you begin talking about blame or consequences at this point, you will probably shut off further conversation.

Do not be too surprised if the individual claims not to remember some or all of what took place. It is not uncommon for people who have lost control to have little or no memory of the incident. In fact, this is one reason people may feel frightened after a crisis — it is alarming to have been so out of control that you do not remember your own actions.

Now it is your turn. Describe the incident from your perspective. If the individual begins interrupting you, remind her that you listened to her side of the story; now it is her turn to listen.

Try to establish basic agreement as to the facts of the incident, but do not expect every detail to mesh. If you have ever read multiple accounts of an incident or accident, you know that people's observations and perspectives vary widely.

PATTERNS

After establishing the basic facts, try to find out why the incident occurred. What triggered it? What were the precipitating factors? Is there a pattern to the person's behavior? Is the acting-out behavior related to time of day, type of activity, medication schedules, or the presence or absence of a particular staff member or peer? Documentation of past incidents can sometimes provide a clue. And do not overlook the obvious: be sure to ask the person if she is aware of any patterns in her own behavior.

If crisis incidents are an almost constant occurrence with this individual, it may be more helpful to look for another type of pattern: when doesn't this person act out? What is different about the times when she is able to control her behavior? When isn't the problem as bad? This also can be helpful information.

INVESTIGATE

In the next step of the CPI COPING Model, both staff and the acting-out individual investigate alternatives to the inappropriate behavior. What other options does the person have? What resources are available to assist her? As in the preceding Pattern stage, it is best if you can involve the individual in identifying her own possible solutions. Encourage her to generate lots of ideas, even things that may seem "off the wall." If you make additional suggestions, do it in a low-key manner by making a comment such as, "Here are some things that other people have tried when they feel like they're ready to hit someone." After you develop a list of possible solutions, work with the person to identify those likely to work best.

Resources can be external, like counseling or classes in anger management, but don't overlook the person's own resources — knowledge, beliefs, motivation, family, and friends.

NEGOTIATE

Using the ideas generated in the Pattern stage, negotiate with the person for some kind of change. Keep in mind that change is not easy for most of us. Patterns of behavior, even when they are unhealthy, become comfortable. Help the person see the positive consequences or benefits of changing her behavior. Use a "small step" approach to change — help the person set realistic goals that will begin building a series of small successes. Most of the people with whom we work have had more than enough failures in their lives.

As you negotiate for change, focus on starting new behaviors, not just stopping old ones. It is easier to get someone to start doing something than to stop doing something else. If you want Mary to stop hitting, what do you want her to do instead? What will replace the old behavior?

Consequences are also discussed at this stage — in terms of both the incident that just occurred and future incidents. It is often a good approach to ask the individual what she thinks the consequences should be if the behavior recurs. You may be surprised at how "tough" people can be on themselves. In any case, be sure that future consequences are spelled out clearly.

You may wish to summarize your understanding with the person through a verbal or written contract. Remember that contracts are more likely to be followed if they are negotiated, not imposed. Give some consideration to your part in the contract.

Contracts are two-sided promises. If a student promises to come to you the next time he is angry and is tempted to hit another student, you must promise to be responsive when he does come to you. If you brush him off and tell him that you have no time to talk with him, he will probably continue to hit. Think about how much of a commitment you are willing to make to help this person change his behavior.

GIVE

The final step in the CPI COPING Model is to give control back to the person who acted out. During the crisis, this person experienced a loss of control. We must return control to the person if we want her to grow.

In addition to control, you need to give the person support and encouragement. You may be the only person who believes that this individual is capable of growing and changing; she may not believe it herself. Self-fulfilling prophecies can be very powerful.

Separate the doer from the deed. Let the person know that you still care for her, although you may not have cared for her actions.

Finally, and perhaps most important, give the person a sense of closure. So often an individual gets labeled as a "problem student" or a "difficult client." Perhaps the best gift we can give someone is a clean slate — a chance to move forward without a dark cloud hanging overhead.

STAFF DEBRIEFING

Another essential part of postvention is staff debriefing. One goal of debriefing is to discuss the facts and procedures surrounding a crisis incident: What happened? How did staff respond? How could the intervention have been better handled? What can be done to prevent a similar crisis in the future? Postvention leads to a focus on prevention.

A second goal of debriefing is to allow staff members to talk about their personal feelings and needs. Sometimes staff may feel angry at the person who acted out — or angry with a co-worker. A staff member may feel embarrassed, or even ashamed, by the way she intervened — if she froze or overreacted, for example. Staff may feel frightened by the seriousness of the incident and afraid that it might happen again. A staff member may be doubting his professional abilities, including his ability to establish a therapeutic relationship with the person who acted out. Because of the potentially sensitive nature of these topics — facts and feelings — it is important that staff debriefing take place in a supportive, nondefensive atmosphere.

Handled appropriately, debriefing can be a tool for growth and improvement. Think in these terms for a moment: A police car is involved in a high-speed chase — reaching top speeds and hitting huge potholes. After, the car does not perform quite the way it used to. Some parts may be in need of adjustment or alignment after traveling such rough roads. In short, it needs a tune-up. Similarly, as human beings, we sometimes need "emotional tune-ups" after being in a crisis situation. If this tune-up or debriefing does not occur, performance is almost sure to suffer.

Just as the CPI COPING Model was used in establishing Therapeutic Rapport, it can be used as a means of organizing a debriefing session by providing an outline to follow. This encourages input and discussion, while at the same time giving the process a sound structure. Keep in mind that the process is designed to be short-term and not overly time consuming. During the debriefing, the facilitator should try to determine if any staff members are in need of follow-up with a trained counselor.

CONTROL

Before staff members can discuss the facts surrounding a crisis situation, they must be back in control. Providing a chance to express their feelings is one way of helping staff to release some of their stress and to regain a sense of control.

It is not always easy for a staff member to admit that she experienced anxiety or lost control during a crisis. She may feel that such an admission is a negative reflection on her professionalism. Acknowledging these feelings as real, healthy, and normal is an important part of the debriefing process.

ORIENT

The second part of the debriefing process consists of establishing the basic facts. What occurred before and during the crisis situation?

Although it is important to hold debriefing sessions in a timely manner, incident reports should be written by all team members before the debriefing session is held. Hearing other people's accounts of an incident can easily change one's own memory of what took place.

Each person in the debriefing session should recreate the crisis in chronological sequence based on what he or she personally saw and heard. At this point, other staff members should not interrupt or even ask clarifying questions. Expect perceptions to vary; each person will have experienced the crisis in a different way.

When everyone has spoken, the group facilitator summarizes the information given, noting areas of agreement as well as any areas of doubt or dispute.

PATTERNS

The next part of the debriefing session entails identifying individual and team behavior patterns that were exhibited during the intervention. Patterns can include those associated with feelings, thoughts, or actions. It is helpful to look at the patterns of the individual team members as well as the overall pattern of the team. By exploring these patterns, you can determine if certain behaviors are helping or hindering your intervention efforts. Some behavior patterns are productive, others are not.

Here are some questions to ask during debriefing to determine which patterns to keep and which to modify or eliminate:

- What were team members thinking and feeling during the crisis? After the crisis?
- How was the team summoned to the scene?
- Was the team summoned at the right time? Too soon? Too late?
- Did everyone know who the team leader was?
- Did the team leader give clear directives?
- Did only one person speak to the acting-out individual?
- Did staff members respond to the acting-out person's behavior?
- Were staff members able to depersonalize the situation and remain rationally detached?
- Was a physical restraint necessary?
- If a physical restraint was used, were the staff members who took part properly trained?
- Was the best possible care, welfare, safety, and security provided to all who were involved?

INVESTIGATE

At the Investigate stage of the CPI COPING Model, staff members are looking for resources and ideas to help prevent the next crisis and to improve the next team intervention. Any problem areas identified in the Pattern stage are examined for possible changes, and the needs of individual team members are also addressed. Resources could include:

- Further debriefing with a trained counselor

- Stress management classes
- Review of crisis intervention procedures
- Crisis response team drills
- Reassessment and possible reassignment of duties

NEGOTIATE

Based on the ideas generated from the Investigate stage, team members now come to an agreement about which ideas to implement and what they will do differently next time. The emphasis is on working together to improve future interventions.

Feedback to team members must be specific and objective if it is going to be helpful in creating change. For instance, if a staff person made a bad situation worse by yelling at a client during an intervention, it is not very helpful to say, "Next time don't overreact." It is more helpful to tell the person, "When John is yelling, you can be certain he has lost some rational control. He probably won't hear what you say to him and yelling back makes the situation worse. It's usually best to keep your distance and let him get it out of his system."

GIVE

After negotiating a plan for the future, it is important for staff members to give each other support and encouragement and to express trust and confidence in one another. During a crisis, staff are faced with many decisions that must be made in a matter of seconds. In hindsight, not every decision will have been the best one. Team members are often their own worst critics if the intervention does not go well.

After an incident has been discussed and a plan developed to improve future interventions, team members need to give one another a sense of closure. They must begin to look forward instead of backward. Clients are not the only ones who can benefit from a clean slate!

SUMMARY

There are only three possible outcomes after a crisis occurs: things get better, things get worse, or things stay about the same. The first outcome is certainly the most desirable, but, without a postvention process, it is probably the least likely.

One part of postvention involves establishing Therapeutic Rapport with the person or persons who acted out. By taking advantage of a narrow window of time after a crisis when people are more amenable to the idea of change, you have an opportunity to facilitate growth and re-establish your therapeutic relationship with the individual.

Staff debriefing is an equally important part of postvention in which staff members discuss the factual, objective part of a crisis incident as well as the emotional, subjective part. Debriefing is a way of improving future team interventions; it is also a way for staff members to take care of themselves. And caring for oneself is the first step in providing care, welfare, safety, and security for others.

CHAPTER SIX

STAFF FEAR AND ANXIETY

IN DISCUSSING THE CRISIS DEVELOPMENT BEHAVIOR LEVELS, we are looking at anxiety primarily from the perspective of the person experiencing the crisis. As staff members, we may also experience anxiety, and even fear, from time to time. Unfortunately, some staff members believe that acknowledging these feelings is admitting to weakness. Others insist that because of their many years of experience, there is no longer anything that frightens them. Neither position is helpful or accurate.

Anxiety and fear are universal human emotions. We may not become fearful and anxious for the same reasons, and we may react in different ways, but we all experience these emotions at some time in some way. Being fearful or anxious need not be a source of embarrassment or shame. Instead, we should recognize that these very real feelings have several beneficial effects which can actually help us keep ourselves and others safe in a moment of crisis.

The Psychology and Physiology of Fear

Often when we think about fear or anxiety, we think of them as emotions that can be controlled through our thought processes. There is some truth in this; the way in which we perceive events and circumstances certainly plays a role in the emotions we experience. However, there is an additional component to fear and anxiety — and that is a physiological one.

When we become frightened, our bodies respond by getting ready to deal with the cause of our fear. This primitive response is part of our "fight or flight" survival instinct. When we feel threatened in some way, our bodies respond without distinguishing the nature of the threat. That is to say, a fear response could be triggered by a person pulling a gun on us — or by our taking a final exam.

In either case, our adrenal glands release epinephrine, more commonly known as adrenalin. Epinephrine increases our blood pressure as well as the strength and rate of our heartbeat. It also causes glycogen in the liver to be converted to glucose, providing a ready source of energy to our muscles. This physiological response can be helpful to us in a crisis situation. Trying to deny or eliminate fear is not only unrealistic, it is undesirable. Our goal is not to get rid of fear and anxiety, but to use them in ways that improve our responses to crisis situations. Fear is a natural physiological reaction to danger. It produces changes in our bodies, giving us the tools to react to the potential threat. The way in which we react and use these additional resources during a crisis can be either productive or nonproductive.

UNPRODUCTIVE RESPONSES TO FEAR AND ANXIETY

Although fear and anxiety can be useful emotions, we can probably think of times when our reactions to them were less than helpful. One common response is to freeze, to become paralyzed like a deer caught in the headlights of an oncoming car. This reaction is akin to the stage fright many of us experienced when performing at a piano recital or in a school play. Crisis moments usually require action. Freezing during a crisis can endanger your safety and the safety of others on the scene.

A second unproductive response to fear and anxiety is overreacting. This can come in many forms, from verbal release to an unwarranted use of physical restraint. In its worst form, it may involve some form of abuse.

A third response to fear and anxiety that we would prefer to avoid is acting inappropriately. Swearing at a student or laughing at a patient who is threatening suicide would be examples of such behavior. The laughter, by the way, does not occur because we think the situation is humorous, but because of the "nervous energy" created by our anxiety.

None of these responses is constructive — which is part of the reason fear and anxiety are considered negative emotions. Keep in mind, however, that the fear itself is neither positive nor negative. Essentially, the person who freezes is experiencing the same internal changes as the person who acts quickly and decisively. The difference is that the decisive person has learned how to channel his or her internal resources into responses that help the situation rather than hinder it.

PRODUCTIVE RESPONSES TO FEAR AND ANXIETY

We have all heard the seemingly impossible stories of people performing unbelievable acts of strength under extreme circumstances, such as lifting a car off a child who has been pinned underneath. Although these accounts sometimes become exaggerated in the retelling, there is some truth to the notion that people under duress — that is, those experiencing fear and anxiety — exhibit increased speed and strength. Epinephrine pumping through their systems does allow them to surpass their everyday abilities.

Another productive response to fear and anxiety is the shortening of our response time. In a fearful situation we are able to mentally evaluate and physically respond to situations much more quickly than usual. This ability to respond quickly is of great benefit in a crisis situation.

Additionally, our sensory acuity increases whenever we are anxious or scared. It is not that we suddenly see better or hear better, but that we make better use of our senses in such circumstances. Imagine walking along a busy downtown street at midday with several friends. Now imagine walking down that same street at two o'clock in the morning — alone. Under which circumstances would you be paying more attention to the people, automobiles, and sounds in your vicinity? The anxiety created by the second scenario would probably result in more sensory awareness of your surroundings.

COPING WITH FEAR AND ANXIETY

Undoubtedly, the productive responses we have described are the ones we all would prefer to experience in moments of crisis. But how can we reduce those ineffective responses and maximize the effective ones? Here are some ideas that will help you.

First, acknowledge what it is that makes you afraid. Are you afraid of being hurt? Of hurting someone else? Of embarrassing yourself by acting inappropriately during a crisis? Of letting down a co-worker? Recognizing your fears and limitations is the first step in dealing with them.

Second, learn how to keep yourself and others safe in a crisis situation. There are nonharmful techniques you can learn for protecting yourself and others, even those who are physically violent. Being prepared in this way will increase your confidence and reduce the likelihood of your responding unproductively.

Finally, don't intervene alone. Whenever possible, use a team approach to crisis intervention. Most of us feel safer, more professional, and more in control when we know we have the support and back-up of other team members. This subject is addressed in much greater depth in the next chapter.

Summary

Fear and anxiety are universal human emotions that can be used to our benefit. By taking steps ahead of time to prepare ourselves, we can capitalize on the productive responses to fear and anxiety and respond more competently in crisis moments. One of the most important steps we can take to help us deal with these emotions is to use a team approach to crisis intervention.

CHAPTER SEVEN

TEAM INTERVENTION

THE WAY WE RESPOND TO A CRISIS has a direct impact on the development and outcome of the situation. When staff members are unable to deal with their own fear and anxiety, they are more likely to respond to a crisis in an unorganized, panicked manner that only makes the situation worse. A person in a crisis is often seeking someone to help him regain control. Staff, therefore, must be in control themselves. This is best accomplished through the use of a crisis response team.

Although different organizations use different names, a crisis response team is any group of two or more people responsible for intervening in situations in which the behavior of an individual or individuals poses a threat to themselves or others. The primary goal of a crisis response team is to maintain the safety of every person involved.

This chapter provides an overview of crisis response teams:

the benefits of a team approach, how to select and train your team, how to get your team on the scene in the event of a crisis, who should be in charge of your team, and what that person's duties are. We also take a look at the role of the team after the crisis is over.

The Benefits of Team Intervention

Because any crisis situation has the potential to turn violent, safety must be the prime consideration. Two or more team members can handle an acting-out individual more safely than one person can. Unless the situation leaves you no alternative, it is best to use a team approach.

With a team, there is less chance of injury for both the other person and yourself. Staff injuries can result in lost work time and worker's compensation claims. According to the National Council on Compensation Insurance, the average cost of a worker's compensation claim for back strain is almost $24,000. But crises resulting in injury are likely to have additional consequences which cannot be measured in dollars.

Staff morale is likely to suffer. Some staff members will respond to reports of injury by becoming more aggressive toward acting-out individuals. Others might hesitate to intervene, even when intervention is necessary for everyone's safety.

Another reason for using a team approach is professionalism. When a crisis situation is handled with a team approach, team members can lend support to one another. This helps prevent staff from perceiving aggressive behavior as a personal confrontation. A team intervention makes it easier to avoid personal power struggles.

The potential for litigation is a third reason for using a team. If litigation should occur as the result of a crisis, having used a team will be to your advantage. First, having another person on the scene provides a witness — it is not a matter of one person's word against another. Next, you are more likely to have used a less restrictive technique than you might have in a solo intervention. And finally, staff are less likely to overreact when a team approach is used.

SELECTING YOUR CRISIS RESPONSE TEAM

When selecting a crisis response team, the natural tendency is to choose the biggest, strongest members of your staff — or those who are the most experienced. In practice, size and seniority are not the best criteria for choosing team members.

There is no standard cast of characters for a crisis response team. Support staff, including secretaries and custodians, should not be overlooked as potential team members. Select members based on their competence, building as diverse a team as possible. A diverse team will provide greater flexibility when responding to unpredictable crisis situations.

The number of people on your crisis response team is another important consideration. No more than five people should be needed for most crisis situations involving one acting-out individual. Using more than five people usually results in confusion and may be perceived as an unnecessary show of force. This intimidation may heighten the anxiety of the individual and cause the person to physically act out. More is not necessarily better where crisis intervention is concerned.

This does not mean, however, that you should train only five staff members for your crisis response team. Not everyone will be on the premises and available to assist in every crisis situation. And remember, you may need to make arrangements for the regular duties of team members to be covered by other staff during the crisis intervention.

TRAINING YOUR CRISIS RESPONSE TEAM

Crisis response team members should receive training in verbal intervention, with an emphasis on learning skills to defuse situations before they become physical confrontations. They should also learn nonviolent physical crisis intervention techniques that are safe and nonharmful for both staff and the aggressive individual. Physical intervention should be taught only as an option of last resort.

Training should include planning and practice for handling crisis situations. Team members' roles should be clearly defined. The decisions you make before a crisis occurs are likely to be more rational than those you make during the actual incident.

One of the best ways to prepare your team for a crisis is to practice. Most facilities conduct fire drills on a regular basis. But a fire is not the only — or even the most likely — type of emergency situation that may occur at your facility. Crisis response drills are equally important. They help ensure the readiness of your team and provide an opportunity to determine, in advance, if any adjustments to your crisis response procedures are necessary. Drills are also a good way to build confidence. Here are some key points for conducting your drills.

Conducting Effective Crisis Response Team Drills

First, keep your drills unannounced. Surprise drills give you a more accurate assessment of how prepared your team is. If your team is newly formed, it might be a good idea to let the members know the day the drill will be held, but not the specific time. After team members are more confident in their abilities, surprise drills can be held.

Write out scenarios for your drills based on actual situations your staff has encountered or is likely to encounter. Ask selected staff members who are not a part of the team to role-play these scenarios.

Instruct team members that they are to respond to the drill just as they would to an actual crisis. Your facility's crisis intervention procedures should be followed, and team members should notify any internal personnel they believe are needed. If appropriate, practice drills should include moving staff and individuals served in your facility to a safe location. Such practice will make everyone more likely to follow directives during an actual crisis situation.

Although you want your drills to be as realistic as possible, be sure the drill is not confused with an actual emergency. If notifying outside responders, such as the police or fire department, make sure to contact these agencies well in advance of the drill and determine their willingness to participate. You may want to post signs saying "Crisis Response Team Drill in Progress" to avoid any confusion within your facility.

After the drill is completed, it is extremely important that team members meet, just as they would after an actual crisis. This debriefing provides an opportunity to review what took place, to fine-tune the team's response, and to examine procedures to see if any changes are necessary.

SUMMONING YOUR CRISIS RESPONSE TEAM

In the event of a crisis, it is crucial that the crisis team be summoned quickly and efficiently. Develop a method of calling for help without drawing a crowd of non-essential personnel.

There are several ways to do this. You can send a bystander to get assistance. A public address system with an inconspicuous code can be used. You may be able to equip your facility with two-way radios, or provide crisis team members with beepers. Some facilities have conveniently located silent alarms or other crisis signalling devices. Even a standard intercom or telephone can be an effective way to summon a team.

The Team Leader

One of the keys to successful intervention is decisive action, and for a team to act decisively, it must have a leader. That leader does not necessarily have to be the staff member with the highest rank or the most seniority. You may choose your team leader based on several different criteria.

Selecting a Team Leader

A reasonable place to start in choosing a team leader is to designate the first person on the scene. That staff member likely has the most information about the crisis and has had the most time to assess the situation and develop a plan of action. Using this method, the team leader will change from one situation to another.

Another good choice for team leader is that team member who has the most confidence and competence. Any human being is apt to be anxious when faced with a crisis situation. Yet some staff members, when properly trained, are going to feel more comfortable than others in the role of team leader. That staff member, the one with the most natural confidence, is a good choice for team leader.

If one of your team members knows the acting-out individual and has an already-established rapport, that personal experience could be the key to helping the individual regain control. This team member is also a natural choice for team leader.

Keep in mind that the person who is the best choice for team leader in one situation may not be the best choice in another situation. Furthermore, the same person does not have to remain team leader throughout an entire intervention. For instance, the first person on the scene might start off as the team leader and then "hand off" the lead to another staff member who has rapport with the acting-out person. The shift can be done subtly through a code word or a nonverbal gesture, but it must be done in such a way that all team members know who the new leader is.

TEAM LEADER DUTIES

The team leader has four specific duties during a crisis. First, the leader must assess the situation. Who is involved? How dangerous is the situation? Are there any weapons? Bystanders? Is outside help necessary? Should law enforcement be summoned?

Next, the leader must formulate a basic plan. Decide what needs to be done to bring the situation to a positive resolution. Determine roles for each team member. Responding quickly is usually crucial; however, taking a few seconds to devise a basic plan is well worth the time spent.

The team leader must direct other team members. Crisis intervention is not the time for building consensus. Firm direction is essential. If team members disagree with the way an intervention is handled, such disputes can be resolved after the crisis is over.

Finally, the team leader — or someone the team leader designates — should talk to the acting-out person. The key is to avoid confusion by having only one person communicate with that individual.

Team Debriefing

As important as good communication and teamwork are to a successful intervention, both are equally important after a crisis. We use the term "postvention" to describe what takes place after a crisis. A part of postvention which is very important to the growth and development of your team is a staff debriefing.

A debriefing is a meeting among crisis team members to discuss the crisis, examine the circumstances that led up to it, analyze ways to improve crisis response, and reduce the frequency, duration, and intensity of future crises. Debriefing also provides an opportunity to discuss feelings about the incident and to build trust, confidence, honesty, and rapport among team members. A model for team debriefing is presented in Chapter Five.

Summary

Perhaps the best reason for using a team approach to crisis intervention is the nature of teams and teamwork. We form teams because we can do more working together than we can working alone. Nowhere is this more true than in team interventions. The synergy of a well-trained team is a benefit to all participants — psychologically, emotionally, and technically. By using a cooperative team of trained individuals, you can increase staff morale, reduce the potential for injuries, build confidence, and enhance the care, welfare, safety, and security of everyone in your facility.

CHAPTER EIGHT

BREAKING UP FIGHTS

THROUGHOUT THIS VOLUME, we have been focusing on the application of the principles of *Nonviolent Crisis Intervention* to individuals who may be approaching or experiencing a crisis. However, as anyone who works in the human service field knows, many of the crisis incidents to which we must respond involve more than one individual. As staff members, we are often called upon to deal with disagreements, arguments, shouting matches, and even physical violence among students, patients, residents, or others for whom we have responsibility. Such situations have great potential for danger.

Breaking up fights does not require a whole new set of skills beyond those we have already discussed. Instead, it simply entails the application of the basic principles of *Nonviolent Crisis Intervention* to a somewhat different situation. In this chapter, we look at why fights occur, how to prevent fights before they reach the physical crisis stage, what verbal techniques exist for intervention in fights, and how to use, as a last resort, Nonviolent Physical Crisis Intervention to break up a fight.

WHY DO PEOPLE FIGHT?

Understanding the cause of a fight can help you design your intervention strategy. Most fights occur for one of four reasons.

The first reason that people fight is to save face. No one likes to feel humiliated, especially in front of one's peers. It is not unusual for people to sacrifice personal safety for the sake of dignity or reputation.

Another source of conflict is defending property or territory. The phenomenon of "fashion crimes" is just one example of fights that involve gaining or maintaining the possession of objects at the expense of safety — or even one's life.

Fear is another reason people fight. Fear is a physiological as well as an emotional response, which can become so great that rationality is impaired. The body's "fight or flight" instinct takes over, and the person responds by either fleeing or fighting.

People also fight to test the pecking order. Jealousy over status can provoke one person to challenge another.

Identifying the reason behind a conflict can be a strong asset in defusing the conflict before it becomes violent. It is especially helpful when the individuals involved are still at the Anxiety Level in the Crisis Development Model.

Preventive Techniques

Anxiety Level

The best time to stop a fight is before it starts. Just as in any crisis episode, you are most likely to be successful if you can intervene at the Anxiety Level. The key here is to recognize the tension between two individuals before it explodes. At the Anxiety Level, individuals may be fidgety. You may observe rapid eye movement, muscle tension, posturing, and other nonverbal indicators of strain. Nervous laughter, sarcasm, and a condescending tone of voice could be other signs of stress between the parties.

The recommended approach for handling the Anxiety Level with two individuals who may be headed for a showdown is no different than it would be with one individual who is experiencing anxiety. Use a supportive approach, focusing on the reason behind the confrontation. Let the participants know that you want to help them solve the problem that exists between the two of them. It is important, however, that staff members not take sides and that they respond in a way which is caring and nonjudgmental.

Defensive Level

Not every fight can be defused at this early level, but many can be. When individuals embroiled in an argument shift to the Defensive Level, your response must also shift — from Supportive to Directive. Because the participants have probably raised their voices, your first task is to gain their attention. Approach calmly and confidently, without rushing into the middle of the situation. Maintain some distance from the potential combatants and create a distraction by raising your voice, dropping a book, or slamming a door. This usually creates a shift in attention from the participants to you. After you have the attention of the individuals, give them simple, clear directions, such as, "That's enough! Stop fighting!" Again, it is important not to take sides.

You may need to set limits with the participants at this time, explaining their options as well as the consequences of their behaviors. Be sure your limits are reasonable and enforceable. If it appears that the conflict cannot be settled peaceably, separate the participants to allow them some time to cool down. In most cases, you will be able to avert a physical confrontation.

KEY STRATEGIES IN EARLY INTERVENTION

There are several keys to preventing fights when intervening at the Anxiety and Defensive Levels. First and foremost, do not ignore a potentially dangerous situation. Anxiety and defensive verbal outbursts can quickly turn to violence. If the circumstances appear volatile, be sure to use a team approach. Also, keep in mind the following points.

Remove others. An audience makes a fight more difficult to manage. Peers make it harder for participants to back down without losing face. In fact, without an audience, the motivation to fight may be lost. In addition, bystanders may take sides, serving as cheerleaders for the opponents. In a worst-case scenario, they may even join in the fight itself.

Avoid rushing into the middle of an argument. Approach calmly and confidently, assuming the CPI Supportive Stance, off to the side and away from both individuals. Before attempting to communicate, create a distraction to get the attention of the participants. Remember that your tone of voice and body language send clearer messages than your spoken words. You should strive to convey control, support, and rationality.

Set firm, fair limits for both parties. Do not take sides. Later, when you are helping the parties to resolve the conflict and trying to maintain your relationship with both individuals, your objectivity will be critical.

The preliminary nonverbal and verbal exchanges that usually occur before a conflict becomes physical are signals for you to intervene. Many times, one or both of the participants do not really want to get entangled in a physical fight. They are actually waiting for you to give them an excuse to walk away. Do not miss the opportunity to provide them with one.

Managing Physical Conflicts

Not every fight can be defused at the Anxiety or Defensive Levels. Sometimes the levels are not easily detectable, escalation occurs very quickly, or staff do not arrive on the scene until after the conflict becomes physical. Managing a fight can be both dangerous and frightening. The first goal is to prevent the participants from hurting each other, but you also need to take care of your own safety. In physically combative episodes, it may not be realistic to prevent all injury, but you can attempt to minimize it.

The first step in managing a physical conflict is to take a few moments to devise an intervention plan. Consider the following factors:

- How many combatants are there?
- What is their size, strength, and energy level?
- Do any of the combatants have weapons?
- Are there objects nearby that could be used as weapons?
- Is there an audience?
- What type of assistance is available?

With so many variables affecting a fight, there is not one standard technique for intervening. But in every case, there are steps you can take to help ensure everyone's safety.

Staff members sometimes believe they are obligated to jump into the middle of a fight in an attempt to stop the conflict. This often results in the combatants redirecting their aggression toward you — which not only jeopardizes your safety, but prevents you from assisting others. Unless participants are lacking in size and strength, do not jump between them.

Do not discount the possibility of a verbal intervention even though the fight has become physical. You may be surprised at how effective verbal intervention can be in stopping even the most violent conflicts.

As we discussed earlier, breaking the concentration of the combatants with an auditory or visual distraction dissipates much of the building energy. By itself, this may not stop a fight, but it can make it easier to verbally intervene by startling the parties into a more rational mode.

Before you attempt your verbal intervention, take note of how the participants are fighting. At the outset, both of them probably are fighting offensively. They may appear equally aggressive. Very soon, however, one of them will be injured, become tired, or realize he is outmatched. This individual will fight more defensively, attempting to block and move away from the aggressor. If you direct your verbal statement to the underdog — "Tom, I want you to stop fighting right now and come here!" — you are actually providing the individual with a face-saving way to end the fight. You are much more likely to be successful in defusing the fight than you would be if you directed the same statement to the aggressor.

There are some additional steps toward safety that you can take during a physical fight — even if you are alone. You can remove onlookers, which enhances their safety and may also serve to defuse the intensity of the fight. To ensure the cooperation of bystanders in leaving the area, it is helpful to have a policy that outlines the consequences for failure to leave the scene of a fight when directed to do so by a staff member. Another safety precaution you can take is to move potential weapons and dangerous obstacles, such as tables or chairs, out of the area.

Beyond these measures, it is important to emphasize that if you find it necessary to physically intervene, you should avoid solo intervention unless there is absolutely no question in your mind that you can manage the size and strength of both combatants. In making such an assessment, remember that it is easy to underestimate an individual's strength due to size, age, gender, or disability. Small individuals, even children, may fight with great intensity. Elderly or developmentally disabled people, even though they may seem uncoordinated, can have remarkable strength and agility when involved in a fight. Some of the most violent fights occur between females. Do not underestimate the danger of a fight simply because the participants are young, old, disabled, or female. Our discussion of physical intervention assumes the use of a team approach.

In a physical intervention, it is helpful to understand the nature of energy output during a fight. An extremely high level of physical and emotional energy is expended. This energy expenditure, however, is not constant. Instead, a person's energy output rises and falls in a series of peaks and valleys.

The most powerful expenditure of energy usually occurs

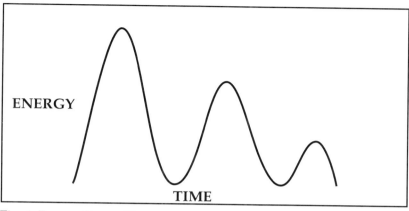

Fig. 4: Energy Expenditure

during the first thirty to sixty seconds of a fight. If you must use physical intervention, avoid the peaks of energy, especially the first one. Instead, wait for a valley. Interventions are much safer during one of the energy lulls.

Unlike the approach used in movie Westerns, it is not advisable for team members to attempt to pry the combatants apart, each team member attempting to restrain a different party. Instead, with two staff members, stay close together and both restrain the more aggressive opponent. The underdog will no longer have anyone with whom to fight and generally will be thankful the fight is over.

Separate the parties as soon as possible. As long as they can see one another, the aggression is likely to persist. Always remember that physical intervention is used as a last resort when it is the only means of providing for the care, welfare, safety, and security of all involved.

AFTER THE FIGHT

The final Crisis Development Level is Tension Reduction. After any fight, whether physical or not, participants experience a state of physical and emotional tension reduction. This may be evident in the form of embarrassment, withdrawal, or even tears. This period of tension reduction is a time when people are more willing to communicate and are more open to change.

The CPI COPING Model discussed in Chapter Five can be used as a guideline for re-establishing communication between the participants. Here are a few key points.

Be sure that you and the parties who took part in the conflict are under control before you attempt to discuss the issue. Allow everyone time and space to regain rationality and composure.

Start by talking to the parties separately. Establish the basic facts and try to get each individual to commit to resolving the issue in an appropriate manner. Try to bring the participants together once they are both rational and have agreed to a meeting. They will feel awkward when they first meet and may be reluctant to communicate. Be supportive and encourage dialogue and problem solving. If an agreement is reached, reinforce it by repeating it or asking them to repeat it. You may even wish to have them sign a written statement to clarify and solidify the agreement.

Outline your expectations and the consequences for any future fights — verbal or physical. Discuss the alternatives to fighting and the positive consequences of appropriate behavior. Give both parties support and encouragement.

SUMMARY

The principles for breaking up fights parallel those which are used when defusing any crisis. The first step is to identify the level of behavior being demonstrated by the parties involved in the conflict. Based on your assessment, you can develop an effective intervention strategy.

At the Anxiety Level of a potential conflict, body language and paraverbal cues tip you off to the tension between two or more individuals. Your Supportive Response is often enough to defuse the situation.

Defensive Level behaviors, such as shouting or cursing, require a Directive Response with clear, enforceable limits.

Actual physical confrontation often can be defused through verbal intervention. If this strategy is unsuccessful, physical intervention may be employed as a last resort. A team approach should always be used, rather than attempting a solo intervention.

Even if you find yourself the only staff member present in a fight situation, you can take several steps to make the environment safer, such as removing onlookers and potential weapons.

After a fight is over and all parties have regained control, it is important to re-establish communication between the involved individuals in an effort to avoid future fights and to create an opportunity for learning and growth.

CHAPTER NINE

RESTRAINT POLICIES

RESTRAINT POLICIES AND PROCEDURES are among the most essential parts of your facility's crisis intervention plan. Putting together carefully crafted polices and procedures can build staff confidence, reduce liability, and uphold the care and welfare of everyone in your facility.

Good policies are not designed to address every conceivable situation a staff member may encounter. That would not be possible, or even desirable. Instead, sound policies are specific enough to provide staff with structure and guidance, but general enough to allow some degree of flexibility and professional judgment.

This chapter addresses some of the key components that should be included in a workable restraint policy. We also address the importance of developing a staff training policy which complements your restraint policy, because — without staff training — your restraint policy will not be workable.

RESTRAINT POLICY RATIONALE AND PHILOSOPHY

The first issue to be addressed in your restraint policy should be an explanation of the philosophy and rationale which underlie your facility's use of restraints. Why do you use restraints? When do you use restraints? What do you hope to accomplish by using restraints? For how long a time period do you physically restrain someone? Here are some key points to consider:

1. In all situations, even those that become physically violent, it is the intent of [*Facility Name*] to provide the best possible care, welfare, safety, and security for all involved.

2. Whenever possible, attempts will be made to prevent or defuse potentially assaultive behavior through early intervention.

3. Physical control and restraint will be used only as a last resort after all verbal intervention efforts have been exhausted and only when the individual presents a danger to self or others.

4. Physical control and restraint will be used only as a temporary measure to take control of another person until that person has regained control of his/her own behavior and is no longer a danger to self or others.

5. Physical intervention is not to be used as a punishment or restriction of freedom, nor will it be used as a means to inflict pain.

PHYSICAL INTERVENTION TECHNIQUES

The next section of your policy should address which physical intervention techniques are authorized for use at your facility. Physical control and restraint sometimes include mechanical restraints, chemical restraints, and involuntary seclusion, in addition to intervention techniques which involve physically holding an individual in some manner.

Your policy should define each technique used and describe the circumstances under which it is employed. In addition, the following statements should be part of every restraint policy:

1. When the need arises for physical control and restraint, the least restrictive techniques, requiring the least amount of force, will be used.

2. Staff members are not to use any form of physical control and restraint for which they have not been trained.

3. The use of physical control and restraint techniques not specifically sanctioned by [*Our Facility*] may be grounds for disciplinary action.

TEAM INTERVENTION

The importance and desirability of team intervention, as discussed in the previous chapter, should be formalized in your restraint policy. Restraint policies and procedures should answer questions such as: Who is on the crisis response team? How is the team summoned? Who is the leader of the team? Under what circumstances are security staff summoned? Under what circumstances are law enforcement personnel summoned?

In addition to answering questions such as these, your policy should include statements similar to the following:

1. It is the policy of [*Our Facility*] to use a team approach to physical crisis intervention whenever possible. Such an approach is the best means of providing for the care, welfare, safety, and security of all involved.

2. Staff members are encouraged to summon team assistance in all situations in which they believe their safety or the safety of others is threatened. Seeking such assistance does not mean that a decision has already been made to physically restrain an individual; rather, it should be seen as a protective safety measure.

3. If physical control and restraint are necessary, the team leader will discontinue the restraint when the out-of-control individual has regained control.

The team leader will then complete a postvention assessment, and due care will be provided for all who were involved in the incident.

STAFF TRAINING

It is imperative that staff members who are responsible for implementing physical control and restraint techniques be well trained, not only in the technical skills required, but also in all policies governing the use of restraints in your facility.

Standards regarding staff training should be part of your restraint policies. Who receives training? How much training do they receive? How soon after staff members are hired do they receive restraint training? How often is the training reviewed?

Your policies also need to address the qualifications of the person who is doing the training. In the case of a copyrighted program such as *Nonviolent Crisis Intervention,* you must be sure that the staff trainer meets not only your internal standards for trainers, but also the external standards of the proprietary organization that owns the training. The Crisis Prevention Institute requires a minimum of twenty-four hours of training, along with other requirements, for its Instructor Certification Program.

The training standards listed below are recommended because we know they have been successful for a wide variety of facilities. Providing less than these minimums may not adequately prepare your staff for their crisis intervention responsibilities.

1. All staff will receive twelve (12) hours of *Nonviolent Crisis Intervention* training within thirty (30) days of employment. A minimum of three (3) hours of refresher training will be provided and required every six (6) months.

2. All staff trained in the use of physical control and restraint techniques will first be trained in verbal and nonverbal de-escalation skills.

3. All staff training will be documented according to facility procedures.

4. All individuals conducting restraint training must be qualified to do so based on training, expertise, and experience, as determined by [*Our Facility*]. In addition, *Nonviolent Crisis Intervention* training must be conducted by a Certified Instructor as defined and authorized by the Crisis Prevention Institute.

DOCUMENTATION AND POSTVENTION

The following policy considerations are related to physical control and restraint, but they may also be covered in your documentation and postvention policies.

All incidents that involve physical control and restraint must be fully documented. Your policies and procedures need to answer questions such as these:

- Who is to document such incidents?
- How soon is the documentation to be completed?
- What form is used?
- To whom is the form given after it is completed?
- Who will obtain statements from witnesses who were not directly involved in the incident?
- Who will obtain a statement from the individual who was physically restrained?

Other questions that need to be addressed in your policies and procedures are related to staff postvention; that is, debriefing. How soon after an incident will a debriefing session be held? Who will convene the debriefing session?

In addition to these specific procedures, consider including the following statements in your restraint policies as they relate to documentation and postvention:

1. All staff members who are involved in an incident requiring the use of physical control and restraint will document the incident.

2. All incidents requiring the use of physical control and restraint will be followed by a postvention meeting for the purpose of staff debriefing.

3. All staff who are involved in physical control and restraint will attend the postvention meeting.

4. Incident Reports must be completed and submitted before the postvention meeting is held. (Timing is extremely important because hearing other people's accounts of an incident can actually change one's memory of the incident.)

SUMMARY

Putting together an effective crisis intervention plan must include the development of sound policies which reinforce your organization's philosophy toward the use of restraints, give explicit direction as to which types of restraint may be used and under what circumstances, support the concept and practice of team intervention, provide for adequate staff training, and complement existing policies regarding documentation and postvention.

CHAPTER TEN

STAFF ATTITUDE: THE FINAL KEY

WHAT DOES IT MEAN to be a human service professional? Often when we think of the word "professional," we focus on the education and experience required to join a professional association or achieve certification or licensure in a particular field. But how often have you seen a "professional" person behave in a very unprofessional way? Often it is not because the person lacks the knowledge needed for her professional position; instead, it is a reflection of her attitude.

The verbal de-escalation skills we have been examining are crucial components in effective crisis intervention. But they are only half the picture. The attitude of staff members — conveyed not only in our words, but also in our nonverbal and paraverbal communication — is often the decisive factor in determining whether or not those intervention skills actually succeed in help-

ing an anxious, defensive, or even physically violent person regain control.

Staff attitude is influenced by a host of factors, including the
population of people with whom we work, attitudes of our co-
workers, the degree of support we receive from our facility's
administration, and personal issues in our own lives. But having a positive outlook ultimately comes down to making the
decision that we can control our own attitude, regardless of the
external factors we face. When we take responsibility for developing and maintaining a positive attitude within ourselves, we
have truly become professionals.

Here are some key concepts that can help you to build a positive, productive, and professional staff attitude.

PRECIPITATING FACTORS

As we have already discussed, crisis situations seldom just
erupt out of nowhere. There is usually a build-up of energy which
precedes the actual crisis moment. And underlying that energy
build-up are one or more causes for the person's behavior. These
internal or external causes of acting-out behavior are called Precipitating Factors.

Precipitating factors come in many different forms. Some are
physiological: insomnia or hunger or pain. Think of how your
own behavior changes when you have had too little sleep or
when you have a severe headache. For a person whose coping
skills may be limited to begin with, factors such as these may

easily be enough to cause an episode of acting-out behavior.

But there are many other precipitating factors. Behavior can be changed by drugs, including alcohol, illegal substances, prescription medication, and even over-the-counter remedies. Psychological disturbances, such as delusions or hallucinations, can cause a person to act out. Other causes of disruptive behavior may be fear, loss of personal power, failure, or the need for attention. Boredom can be a precipitating factor, but so can changes in routine or excess stimulation.

As staff members, we have little control over many of the causes of acting-out behavior. Sometimes we do not even know which factor or factors are at work in a given situation. But we do know that we are often seen as safe and convenient targets for the person who has become disruptive, even assaultive.

So how do precipitating factors assist us in building a positive staff attitude? There are at least two important lessons we can learn from looking at precipitating factors.

BECOMING PROACTIVE

Although it is true that we cannot control many precipitating factors, sometimes it is possible to eliminate or ameliorate their effects through a proactive approach.

Teachers whose schools lack breakfast programs could provide graham crackers and juice to hungry children in the morning, knowing that simply allaying their hunger will reduce upsets in the classroom.

Boredom can be reduced by increased programming or the teaching of independent leisure skills. Fear of the unknown can be lessened by explaining procedures and sharing information. Medications can be prescribed for pain, opportunities for choice and control can be extended, and the rate of change can be moderated.

Preventing crisis situations by addressing precipitating factors may create more work for us in the short run, but doing so will, in the long run, be a positive step for the people in our charge — and for ourselves.

DEPERSONALIZING

Understanding precipitating factors can help us in another way. By recognizing that we are seldom the cause of acting-out behavior, we learn the importance of depersonalizing — that is, not taking acting-out behavior as a personal attack. If we remind ourselves that we are simply safe and convenient targets, it is easier to hear slurs about our gender, race, ethnicity — even about our mothers — without being drawn into a verbal battle.

This does not mean that unpleasant behavior should not have consequences. That is a policy issue within each facility. But regardless of your facility's policy, it does little good to take such "button pushing" comments personally. When you do, you allow the other person to gain control over your interaction.

Reminding ourselves (perhaps through internal "self-talk") that we are not really the issue will help us to maintain a professional attitude. If we are not able to depersonalize, we run the very real risk of making a bad situation worse. In fact, we ourselves may become a precipitating factor. If we do not wish to become part of the problem, it is important that we learn to depersonalize. Another name for depersonalizing is Rational Detachment.

RATIONAL DETACHMENT

Rational Detachment refers to the ability to stay in control of one's own behavior and not take acting-out behavior personally. Although we may not be able to control the causes of acting-out behavior, we can control our responses to it.

As caregivers, each of us must develop strategies that will allow us to remain calm and in control during crisis situations. These strategies should include approaches to use before, during, and after a crisis moment.

BEFORE THE CRISIS

Having a plan for handling crisis situations is extremely important. Decisions made before a crisis occurs are likely to be more rational than those made in the midst of a crisis situation. Thinking through a plan of action also gives you confidence, making you less likely to panic during an actual crisis moment.

Developing a team approach should be part of your crisis response strategy. Who can you call upon to back you up when a crisis occurs?

Think about the things that really "set you off" and cause you to lose control. The people with whom we work often know which buttons to push with which staff members. Practice a calm, professional response ahead of time.

DURING THE CRISIS

Remember that you are probably not the true target of the behavior you are seeing. Give yourself positive self-talk, such as, "I know what I'm doing. I can handle this situation. This isn't really about the two of us; it's about other issues in his life."

A nurse in a neonatal intensive care unit related that many times parents verbally attack nursing staff members for trivial items, such as claiming that a diaper has been put on incorrectly. At such moments, this nurse reminds herself that these parents are terrified their tiny, sick infants are not going to survive, and that she is simply an accessible target for their feelings of fear and powerlessness. It doesn't make the insults pleasant to hear, but it does allow her to maintain a calm, professional attitude.

It is also important to recognize one's own limits during a crisis situation. Some of us have the mistaken idea that being a professional means we can handle any situation that comes our way. This is an unrealistic expectation. We are human beings, and as all human beings, we have a breaking point. What distinguishes the true professional is the ability to recognize the point at which we can no longer be effective caregivers. Sometimes the most professional course of action we can take is to step aside and let someone else take over.

AFTER THE CRISIS

When the crisis is over, be sure you find a positive outlet for the emotions you have experienced but may not have been able to release. Talk to your co-workers about the fear or anger you may have felt.

Debriefing with other team members is also important. This is a time to analyze your response to the crisis and begin to plan ways to improve your next intervention.

THE INTEGRATED EXPERIENCE

When we respond to a person who is anxious by becoming anxious ourselves, we only add to the individual's anxiety. When we respond defensively to a person at the Defensive Level of crisis development, we heighten that individual's defensiveness. The concept of the Integrated Experience is that our behaviors and attitudes have an impact on the behaviors and attitudes of those for whom we are caregivers.

If we develop and maintain a positive staff attitude, it is easier for us to stay calm and in control when we encounter a disruptive individual. We can then display positive actions that do not escalate the person's behavior and may assist that individual in regaining control.

SUMMARY

While skills and knowledge are important, staff attitude is an equally significant key to successful crisis intervention. It is important for us as caregivers to be aware that many precipitating factors may lead to acting-out behavior. In some cases, we can take preventive steps to reduce the causes of such behavior. But even when we cannot control the causes, we can control our responses to them.

Rational detachment is the ability to depersonalize a crisis situation by staying calm and in control. Each of us must develop our own strategies for rationally detaching before, during, and after crisis moments.

Crisis development is an integrated experience. This means that we play a key role in influencing the outcome of each crisis situation. Staying in control and expressing a positive attitude allow us to offer the best possible care and welfare for the individuals in our facilities.

CPI
GLOSSARY OF TERMS

Acting-Out Person - the total loss of control which often results in a physical acting-out episode. It is the third Crisis Development Behavior Level.

Anxiety - a noticeable increase or change in behavior. A nondirected expenditure of energy; e.g., pacing, finger drumming, wringing of the hands, or staring. It is the first Crisis Development Behavior Level.

Challenge Position - a body position in which one individual is face-to-face, toe-to-toe, and eye-to-eye in relation to another individual. This position is often perceived as a challenge and tends to escalate a crisis development situation.

Crisis Development Behavior Levels - a series of recognizable behaviors which may escalate to a physical acting-out episode.

Defensive Behavior Level - the beginning stage of loss of rationality. At this stage an individual often becomes belligerent and challenges authority. It is the second Crisis Development Behavior Level.

Directive Staff Attitude - an approach in which a staff member takes control of a potentially escalating situation by setting limits. It is the recommended staff response to defensive behavior.

Due Care - the general duty of care owed to anyone involved in an incident.

Incident - any out-of-the-ordinary occurrence that results in injury, property loss or damage, use of physical force or restraint involving employees, visitors, or individuals in your charge.

Integrated Experience - the concept that behaviors and attitudes of staff impact on behaviors and attitudes of clients, and vice versa.

Kinesics - the nonverbal message transmitted by the motion and posture of the body.

Limit Setting - a verbal intervention technique in which a person is offered choices and consequences. Limits should be clear, simple, reasonable and enforceable.

Nonviolent Crisis Intervention® - a safe, nonharmful behavior management system designed to aid staff members by maintaining the best possible care and welfare for agitated or out-of-control individuals even during their most violent moments.

Nonviolent Physical Crisis Intervention - safe, nonharmful control and restraint techniques to safely control an individual until he can regain control of his behavior. Nonviolent physical crisis intervention is used only as a last resort when a person is a danger to self or others.

Paraverbal Communication - the vocal part of speech, excluding the actual words one uses. Three key components of paraverbal communication are tone, volume, and cadence of speech.

Postvention - a process that occurs after a crisis.

Postvention Assessment - an immediate evaluation of the condition of all who have been involved in an incident to determine the need for medical care or other intervention.

Precipitating Factor - an internal or external cause of an acting-out behavior over which a staff member has little or no control.

Proxemics - personal space. An area surrounding the body, approximately 18 to 36 inches in length, which is considered an extension of self.

Rational Detachment - the ability to stay in control of one's own behavior and not take acting-out behavior personally.

Supportive Staff Attitude - an empathic, nonjudgmental approach attempting to alleviate anxiety. It is the recommended staff response to anxiety behavior.

Supportive Stance - suggested body position for a staff member to maintain when intervening with a potentially out-of-control or acting-out individual. The supportive stance is maintained by keeping a distance of one leg length from the person and by remaining at an angle to that person.

Tension Reduction - a decrease in physical and emotional energy which occurs after a person has acted out, characterized by the regaining of rationality. It is the fourth Crisis Development Behavior Level.

Therapeutic Rapport - an attempt to re-establish communication with an individual who is in the tension reduction stage.

INDEX